Alzheimer

of related interest

Dancing with Dementia
My Story of Living Positively with Dementia
Christine Bryden
ISBN 1 84310 332 X

The Simplicity of Dementia
A Guide for Family and Carers
Huub Buijssen
ISBN 1 84310 321 4

Understanding Dementia
The Man with the Worried Eyes
Richard Cheston and Michael Bender
ISBN 1 85302 479 1

Hearing the Voice of People with Dementia
Opportunities and Obstacles
Malcolm Goldsmith
Preface by Mary Marshall
ISBN 1 85302 406 6

A Guide to the Spiritual Dimension of Care
for People with Alzheimer's Disease
and Related Dementia
More than Body, Brain and Breath
Eileen Shamy
Foreword by Richard Sainsbury, Robert Baldwin and Albert Jewell
ISBN 1 84310 129 7

Alzheimer

A Journey Together

Federica Caracciolo

Foreword by Luisa Bartorelli

Jessica Kingsley Publishers
London and Philadelphia

First published in 2003 in Italian by Carocci editore S.p.A., Roma
as *Alzheimer: Un viaggio in due.*

This edition first published in 2006
by Jessica Kingsley Publishers
116 Pentonville Road
London N1 9JB, UK
and
400 Market Street, Suite 400
Philadelphia, PA 19106, USA

www.jkp.com

Copyright © Carocci editore S.p.A., Roma 2003
Translation copyright © Federica Caracciolo 2006

The right of Federica Caracciolo to be identified as author of this work has been asserted by
her in accordance with the Copyright, Designs and Patents Act 1988.

Library of Congress Cataloging in Publication Data

Caracciolo, Federica.
[Alzheimer. English]
Alzheimer : a journey together / Federica Caracciolo ; foreword by Luisa Bartorelli.— 1st
pbk. ed.
        p. cm.
Previously published in Italian.
ISBN-13: 978-1-84310-408-7 (pbk. : alk. paper)
    ISBN-10: 1-84310-408-3 (pbk. : alk. paper) 1. Caracciolo, Federica. 2. Care-
givers—Italy—Biography. 3. Alzheimer's disease—Patients—Italy—Family relationships. I.
Title.
    RC523.2.C3713 2006
    362.196'831'0092—dc22

                                        2005017635

British Library Cataloguing in Publication Data
A CIP catalogue record for this book is available from the British Library

ISBN-13: 978 1 34310 408 7
ISBN-10: 1 84310 408 3

Printed and Bound in Great Britain by
Athenaeum Press, Gateshead, Tyne and Wear

There are more than 600,000 people
suffering from Alzheimer's disease in Italy.
Francesco was one of those.
These pages are dedicated to them all.

Acknowledgment

Special thanks to Diana Cook for editing the manuscript and for her valuable suggestions and insight.

Contents

Foreword

Among the various experiences published by people living close to an Alzheimer patient, this book strikes me as being one of the most positive. It gives voice to the hope that, despite the suffering, the physical and emotional pain, the inevitable decline of the loved one, the carer can still find some rewards as well as practical solutions when dealing with the recurring and often unforeseeable problems related to the progress of the disease, through a learning process, a degree of creativity and a great deal of love.

In addition to the author's ability to express this deeply positive attitude, she lucidly describes the story of this dramatic 'journey' in a sober and restrained manner that instantly touches the heart – and not only of those personally involved, but also of those aware of this new social problem and who wish to offer their solidarity. In our modern society, in fact, Alzheimer's disease, as well as other forms of dementia, have engaged the attention of health and social services, not least due to the vast numbers of people affected – resulting from an ageing population – but also because this progressively debilitating disease requires enormous organizational efforts and a great deal of technical and human resources. Those who are involved in such services, as well as those who are socially committed, will therefore find in this book occasion for personal meditation and food for thought. Those now living or who have lived through similar situations will, within these pages, certainly find their own experiences reflected.

After her husband's death, a sense of nostalgia for the happy times enjoyed together pervades the author's narration, but also for the darkest hours of the illness which in her memories are tinged with a profoundly human meaning.

The book begins with a meeting of the support group organized to help families of Alzheimer patients in the geriatric ward of Sant'Eugenio Hospital in Rome, where the author, at one time a wife in search of help for her husband, now works as a volunteer. This change of parts shows us how pain can turn into a source of knowledge and take on a meaningful role.

Then, before our eyes, pass the various phases of the illness: from the first denial to its inevitable ending, with all the related cognitive and behavioural symptoms described in their brutal but sometimes perhaps even bizarre reality.

It can be added that the book itself is very pleasingly written. We can appreciate its sincerity, the discretion with which the most harrowing situations are described, broken up by the moments of respite afforded by the intervals dedicated to the memories of travels enjoyed by the couple in Third World countries. Finally, there is the overwhelming *truth* which pervades every page of the narrative.

Luisa Bartorelli
Chief Geriatrician
Sant'Eugenio Hospital, Rome

Chapter One

I park the car outside Sant'Eugenio Hospital in Rome and thread my way through the crowd of visitors, doctors and patients in pyjamas and dressing gowns, all enjoying a breath of fresh air. Ambulance sirens are wailing in the distance. I enter the large, stark and dismal hall and head towards the geriatric ward.

Today, as on every first Thursday of the month, the support group organized for the relatives of Alzheimer patients meets here. There are more people than usual and I see many new faces. At the start of the meeting, newcomers are always invited to speak. Some are ready to talk, others prefer silence, reluctant to describe their hardships in front of so many strangers. People of all ages are gathered together with the same aim: how best to deal with the Alzheimer patient, how best to answer his needs without losing one's sanity, how to cope with the moments of discouragement, helplessness or even merely irritation in the face of persistent irrationality, how to carry out the daily tasks without offending the sufferer's dignity, and how not to despair at the sight of a loved one inexorably slipping away a little more each day. These are the problems which a family must face and there is infinite pain in the eyes of those present, yet coupled with a desire to continue hoping.

Sometimes a spouse or a son or daughter hesitates to ask questions, fearing to lose their remaining illusions, clinging to the hope that the disease might only be a passing one and that the patient might soon improve. At other times there is a need to speak, to ask, to know how others have overcome the ordeal, to claim that one's own problems are greater, and it seems that the torrent of words will never stop because hidden in these outbursts are also to be found the first seeds of resignation and acceptance.

If the problems seem to be similar in every case, the manner of coping with them changes, because each attitude reflects the personality of the individual concerned. But the aim is identical: getting close up to this new dimension: dementia.

The situation is viewed differently by a son or a daughter than by a spouse. Young people seek practical solutions, their approach is more objective, they do not want to sacrifice their own lives. On the contrary, the spouse is more deeply involved, he deplores the change he notes in the other's feelings, suffers from the unexpected indifference, is wounded by the hostility shown. But there is also talk of a new relationship where roles are reversed, of the joy and the tenderness caused by a sudden recognition, a smile.

I am here today as a volunteer: I have experienced all these problems at first hand. I too have thought like so many of those present 'I wish all this could end, I wish I could regain the serenity I had before'. But the disease changes us deeply. That 'before' will never return. Instead a very special relationship is established with the patient, composed of infinite patience and compassion. One discovers a new capacity to give, to love, and often one emerges from this strange battle not conquered but a conqueror.

I remember my first visit here, seven years ago, at the beginning of Francesco's illness. There were many of us that day also, but I was part of the group. Then, as they were, I was worn out with anxiety, deeply conscious of my helplessness and afraid.

Life has now changed for me. My journey is over but I can perhaps be of some help to others. This is why I am about to tell my story, which, in many ways, is not unlike that of so many others.

Chapter Two

I cannot say exactly when I noticed that matters were not going well with Francesco. There were scattered episodes of growing inattention, an increasing forgetfulness, the inability to follow even a simple argument, an almost maniacal obsessiveness over some things. They were signals, no doubt, but signals to which I did not wish to give too much importance, perhaps wanting to refute the signs of incipient ageing, or at least those that I attributed to age, because our life had been one of continuous vitality, of unceasing activity where the present served to plan the future.

We were both passionately fond of travelling and we had travelled so much together, starting with our first trip to Romania, during Easter week, many years before, shortly after we met. Francesco had a Fiat 1200 at the time and we took to the road in our open car heading towards the Danube delta, happy to enjoy the first spring sunshine and to savour new aromas, eager not to miss anything of the places we visited. We slept wherever the road took us, sometimes in so-called luxury hotels, sometimes in the houses of strangers, with many of whom we subsequently established a wonderful friendship.

Soon after that first trip, Francesco had wanted to equip his old camper, an ancient ambulance from the time of the Second World War, and transform it into a desert-going vehicle. Like the competent interior architect he was, he attended to every detail so that our long journey over rough tracks would be as comfortable as possible. Nothing was left to chance. With this vehicle we crossed the Sahara three times. Then there were our journeys to various countries of Central Africa and Asia. After that it was the turn of Canada and America.

Francesco was always spurred on by his overwhelming need to keep on the move, by his ever-renewed joy in cutting loose from his roots, by his enthusiasm in facing each new page of his life still to be written. Freedom and independence were the top priorities in his scale of values.

And I too had been infected. Preparing our luggage had become one of my pet tasks, because it was not just a case of choosing clothes for a few days or weeks, but for months or even a year, and they had to be packed in special containers.

It was perhaps in this context of travel that I began to notice the first symptoms of the disease, in that slowly but inexorably his desire to leave home was diminishing and our trips became shorter and shorter.

Following after Africa, Asia and America, our furthest targets had been Egypt and Greece. Then only Italy. And finally we did not travel by camper anymore but by car, sleeping in hotels. Our final trip was by train.

THINKING BACK NOW at a distance of some years, it seems to me that this is exactly when I began to notice a subtle change, the insidious beginnings of a precariousness that in a short while turned into dependence, later to become total.

Chapter Three

Each year I went to Egypt to visit my mother, the only member of my family who had stayed on in Alexandria, despite the revolution, the confiscation of our property following the land reform, and the rising hostility towards foreigners, particularly Jews. Like many of those of her generation, my mother was at home in Egypt despite not being an Egyptian national, rooted like a tree even when it seemed that the ground was about to be swept from under her feet.

On my last visit there I had felt unhappy at the thought of leaving Francesco in Rome. But I knew that my absence would not be for more than ten days and, I have to admit, the thought of a short holiday on my own was pleasing. So I put aside my emerging worries.

However, Francesco had placed a condition on my departure: there was to be no air travel. After our last trip to Africa he had been left with the traumatic memory of our return aboard a small Congo Airlines plane which, caught up by the monsoon wind, had buffeted us around for two hours in the sky above a vast expanse of rainforest while blinding flashes of lightening split the sky above our heads. 'No more flying', he had decreed peremptorily. And so for this trip I had chosen to travel by the slowest but also the most attractive of means: by ship.

I was happy at the prospect of spending two days at sea and of feeling once more, after many years, the emotion of arriving at Alexandria by ship. Just as during my childhood voyages, the first signs of approaching land were the palm trees, silhouetted against the intense blue of the sky, looking as though they had risen, one by one, out of the boundless expanse of sand and dunes on the east side of the city.

Immediately after, the sparkle of the golden dome of the old royal palace of Ras-El-Tin, and finally the shouts of the porters eager to be the first to grab our luggage and to earn a large *bakshish* for their services.

I thought with anticipation of the fragrance of the grilled kebabs and fried falafels which would waft from the small traditional Arab restaurants in the city suks, and recalled the aroma of *bukhur*, the incense burning in braziers hung from a ring which the beggars swing under the noses of the passers-by in the hope of getting a piastre in exchange for promised good luck, all so characteristic of that Mediterranean shore where I was born.

MY MOTHER LIVED in an attractive penthouse in central Alexandria with terraces from which one could glimpse the sea. It was not our old family house – a villa with a large garden that had been sold during the difficult period that followed Nasser's rise to power – and very little of the furniture and ornaments that still peopled my childhood memories remained, but it enjoyed a wonderful position and was very close to the places I intended to revisit.

The city centre had not changed in any great way over the years since I had left. Time's patina had blurred its lines, dimmed its features, as happens with some people seen again after many years, when age has made their gaze less bright, dulled the shine of their hair, slightly slowed down their gait but so subtly that one hesitates to mention ageing and says only, 'I found them a bit changed'.

While walking along the old Canopic way, which today is the Attarine district, I was struck again by the surprising number of churches: Armenian, Greek, Orthodox, Greek–Syrian, Greek–Catholic, Latin, Maronite, Presbyterian, Methodist, Anglican as well as the synagogue, and finally the huge Coptic church enclosed in a small square behind a monumental iron gate, painted black, and surrounded, like the backcloth of a stage, by narrow buildings squeezed together, from whose windows, floating like so many flags, hangs the washing of an entire neighbourhood. This was Alexandria, the multicultural, multiethnic and polyglot city that had forged the personalities of all those who were born and grew up there.

My pilgrimage had taken me later to the meeting places of my adolescence, the pastry shops, Pastroudis, Athineos, *Le Petit Trianon*, where the community of Greek entrepreneurs predominates, and finally the Elite, a historic restaurant patronized by all Alexandrians and that in my time strove to appear as an orientalized version of the Parisian café 'Les deux magots' because of the assiduous presence of painters, writers, musicians and other artists.

Returning from my stroll, just as I entered the flat, I could hear the telephone ringing. It was Francesco who, in a state of great anxiety, wanted to know the date and hour of my return, which we had in fact agreed upon together long before my departure. During my stay in Alexandria, these calls were repeated many times a day, sometimes with intervals of barely fifteen minutes. Once the telephone even rang at dawn. Suddenly woken up I thought at first that it was part of some local event, typical of the Bairam period, the great Muslim feast which follows the long fast of Ramadan. Then full consciousness returned. 'Oh my God, the telephone', I realized as I jumped out of bed, 'and worse still it's in my mother's room.' Fortunately, being a little deaf, she heard nothing. Francesco's voice was strangled with anxiety. 'There's been a burglary. They've emptied the safe, I can't find our money!' I felt faint. Then I began to think clearly. 'Did you find the safe open?' I asked. 'No.' 'Have they broken down the door? Go and see.' The door was undamaged so no one had broken in. I advised him to close the safe and go back to bed. Later in the day his tone of voice seemed normal. We did not mention the incident again but the telephone continued to ring without respite throughout the next ten days.

MY RETURN JOURNEY, again by ship, allowed me two days of peace and reflection before having to face the problems again with decision. But on board there was also a telephone and it seemed to ring only for me. One day when the sea was a little choppy, I was imprudent enough to tell Francesco that the ship was rolling a bit, but to calm his immediate concern I added that it did not worry me as I did not suffer from seasickness, as well he knew after our many transatlantic voyages. I thought I had reassured him. However, during the afternoon, while I was sunbathing at the edge of the pool, the ship's loudspeaker began broadcasting a message. At first I listened to it absentmindedly then, suddenly, I heard my name spoken with a request to present myself immediately at the purser's office. I quickly ran down the steps that led to the passengers' reception.

The young officer on duty looked me up and down for what seemed an extraordinarily long time and then, in a slightly sarcastic tone, asked me how I felt. 'Very well, thank you. Why?' I asked, taken aback at this unexpected interest, but quickly understood that there had to be some more serious reason behind this. 'Your husband has telephoned. He said that, owing to your bad state of health, he would like an ambulance to be ready for you tomorrow when we arrive at Bari.'

I was aghast. I immediately telephoned Francesco to beg him to stop his absurd worrying, but while I was speaking I was overcome by a dark foreboding and I spent the rest of the day in a state of deep turmoil.

A few minutes after berthing, I saw Francesco waiting together with the police. As soon as he could get on board he flew towards me, beside himself, a look of bewilderment in his eyes. Hiding my embarrassment, I took him to my cabin and tried to appease him.

Later, once he had calmed down, we spent a quiet afternoon in Bari, strolling along the sea front which reminded me of Alexandria, Salonica and many other seaside Mediterranean cities.

Once we were back in Rome, my daughter, Micaela, telephoned me from Ferrara, where she lives, to express her dismay. 'Did you know that Francesco called me every day?' And he had done the same with all our friends. I understood that in that state of rising insecurity, the loneliness had been unbearable for him and he had been desperately seeking support.

The neurologist, whom I immediately consulted on my return, tried to reassure me. 'What do you expect? Your husband is over seventy, and it's normal at that age to lose a bit of memory.' It did not seem at all normal to me, also because on our return I had found the apartment in a shambles: the bed unmade, the sofa covered with crumpled sheets, the walls pasted with dozens of pieces of paper bearing the date of my return to Rome in ever larger letters.

THE REST OF the year, however, passed without any other significant incident. Francesco's memory dwindled more, but I was becoming used to substituting it with my own. Our daily routine did not change much; I continued with my translations and Francesco – temporarily without work – divided his time between designing on the computer and reproducing cuttings taken here and there from public gardens and for which he had made a kind of greenhouse complete with fluorescent lighting.

What really worried me was that these activities, carried out in the past as a diversion between one job and another, were taking on an obsessive nature.

Also, his behaviour towards me had changed: he continually asked with ever greater insistence for proofs of my affection and expressed his with an intensity at times frightening. It became increasingly difficult to arrange meetings with my friends or to go out alone as on my return I invariably found Francesco in the middle of the road, overcome by panic if I was even a minute late.

Chapter Four

We had a house in the country a few kilometres from Zagarolo, near the Roman Hills, at the foot of a small hill on which stood the town of Gallicano nel Lazio.

We had bought it, charmed by this secluded little town which appeared suddenly at the mouth of a deep gully cut into the tufa: it gave us the impression of entering into an ancient world still untouched by the waves of holidaymakers who had invaded the surrounding villages. A thick wood encircled the area, accentuating the seclusion: one entered almost on tiptoe. The house we chose also stood amidst a sea of green. It needed a complete renovation and this was precisely why Francesco had fallen in love with it. As soon as it was ours, we had moved in with our camper and parked on the large terrace in front of the house and there, in the summer evenings, we spent many hours enjoying the night scene of the little town that we could catch glimpses of through the trees, twinkling like a Christmas tree, while we made our renovation plans. When night fell the woods filled with a thousand sounds. We watched in silence the reawakening of the hidden life that escaped our attention in day time. We saw snakes mating, the darting of fireflies like so many shooting stars, a family of weasels that later became almost domesticated and took over a corner of the garden, moving around quite undisturbed. One night I found myself face to face with a fox. Its eyes, two points of light that stabbed the night, saw me turned to stone, holding my breath. But the flight was immediate. Every species of bird populated our garden and the surrounding woods, in particular one that especially delighted me because every morning at dawn it whistled a theme from Beethoven's Pastoral Symphony. And of course, at every moment of the day, the deafening chirrup of the cicadas making the whole garden throb, the sudden silences alternating with the miraculous resumption in unison of their song. It was our enchanted garden.

This is where Francesco's great passion for plants began and he nurtured them with enormous devotion. In fact, after only a few years, our garden contained hundreds of bushes and trees that had been planted entirely by us. When we arrived, apart from a clump of dahlias left by the previous owner, the house was surrounded by a vast expanse of unkempt land.

It was also in Gallicano, one summer, that I noticed new signs of Francesco's illness. Always so dextrous with his hands, he who had transformed our apartment in Rome with exquisite taste into a Palladian palace, was unable to nail together the four pieces of wood that were to be the base of a small corner cabinet. Every measurement taken was cut badly and no lengths corresponded to the measurements taken. I watched the sequence of errors with increasing concern and noticed with deep pain his anger and frustration when, at the end of a day's hard work, invariably the cabinet collapsed. I noticed also the first signs of a great desperation that he tried to hide so as not to admit to himself, nor to me, his failures, because only a short time before he had built on his own a large bookcase in our house in Rome and another just as large in Gallicano. Those bookcases were his pride and joy, and here a whole summer had not sufficed to finish off a corner cabinet.

These episodes, however, were not frequent enough to disturb me greatly, so in September of that year we decided to take a short holiday, choosing this time to travel by train. In fact for some time, even though he loved the car, Francesco was uncertain and distracted at the wheel and I had to insist on driving.

The change in his surroundings accentuated his problems and his irrationalities and the moments of bewilderment multiplied. In the hotel bathroom in Vicenza, he was amazed to see 'through the port-hole' that the trees were not moving. 'This ship is never going to put out to sea!' he exclaimed angrily. I tried to bring him back to reality, the reality that I believed was the only one, not realizing that his was already very different and that we were communicating on two wavelengths, widely apart.

In Verona one night there was an episode of incontinence and a desperate search for the bathroom – which was adjacent to our room – in the corridors of the lower floors of the hotel. I still tried to convince myself that these were isolated incidents. Perhaps he had had a little too much to drink the evening before. Perhaps in his drowsiness he was a bit confused. Perhaps … but I also began to feel the first real anxiety.

In Milan, staying as guests with some friends for whom Francesco had designed a splendid apartment in the city centre, creating an authentic hanging garden on the terrace, I tried to play down the lapses and forgetfulness. Our friends wished to move to Rome and delegated Francesco to find them an apartment and restructure it. I understood perfectly well that he was no longer able to take on such a responsibility. In fact, his capacity for concentration was considerably diminished: already the previous year he had been unable to remember the names of the workmen and the appointments he had made with them, so much so that the clients had to halt the work halfway through the renovation process.

Chapter Five

It was October once again, time for my departure for Alexandria, at the tail end of the stifling summer heat. This time I decided to take Francesco with me. My mother had moved to an old people's home which also offered comfortable accommodation for visiting guests. Initially Francesco was opposed to the idea. 'Why don't you ask your mother to come to Rome instead?', he asked, he who adored Alexandria and always dreamed of returning there. But our plans could not be altered. My mother had left her apartment for good and had to sell all her furniture; so my presence was essential. Plus I was counting on Francesco who, as an expert designer, could help us to value the objects and settle the prices.

But things went wrong even before we left. The key to the small safe, which contained our passports, air tickets and money, had suddenly disappeared. Searching through all the drawers, cupboards and cabinets of the house did not bring it to light. For years we had kept this key in a hiding place well known to us both, and now suddenly it appeared to have been moved. I called Irene, our young Polish cleaning girl, counting on her precision and meticulousness to help us in the search. Together we went very carefully through every corner again but to no avail. There was no other alternative but to request the locksmith to come and break open the safe.

We departed, leaving an enormous hole in the wall, while within me awakened a dark foreboding.

AT THE EGYPTIAN customs our luggage, together with that of the other passengers, had been piled helter-skelter into some huge wheeled metal containers. While I observed with great dismay the chaotic extraction of our suitcases, Francesco looked around him perplexed. 'The Italians have gone mad, all the ads are in Arabic now!' Concentrating on keeping our luggage in sight, I made the mistake of not giving enough importance to his remark which should, instead, have aroused grave suspicions in me.

The old people's home was immersed in a large and luxuriant garden – an absolute miracle in a city where water is always scarce – with an adjacent orchard overflowing with tropical plants. Francesco seemed relaxed and happy surrounded by so much vegetation, and I drew a sigh of relief.

In the guest house we had been given two comfortable rooms and while I prepared to unpack our cases, Francesco announced his intention to go down into the garden again, wander round once more, and perhaps go and look 'at that house with the strange dome on the other side of the road'. 'Don't go out', I enjoined, worried because I knew that Alexandria was still for him an unknown city, despite his former visit. He reassured me and I saw him go down the stairs with the small bag containing our passports round his neck. 'Go first to the reception and leave our passports', I added, worried that they might get lost.

Having taken over our rooms and hung up our clothes, I pulled a deck-chair towards the end of the balcony overlooking the sea and sat down to enjoy the warm autumn sun. I even fell asleep, waking up only when I heard voices coming from beneath the large ficus tree which was throwing its long afternoon shadow over the sun-bathed lawn. Good, I thought, Francesco has already made friends, and I was about to resume my sleep when a second thought made me bounce to my feet. It could not be Francesco down there, because he was wearing sandals and the person whose feet I caught a glimpse of there below was wearing shoes. I rushed down the stairs; and in fact Francesco was not there nor, after a rapid inspection, was he to be found in the garden. Nobody had seen him at the Reception.

IT IS STILL difficult for me today to describe the horror of those hours which followed Francesco's disappearance. Many times I thought I would lose my mind during the two days of his absence. I remembered with dismay and a deep sense of guilt that he did not speak the local language and that perhaps he had never realized that he was no longer in Italy; and now, through my negligence, he was lost. Nothing was brought to light by my ever-widening exploration around the home, by the questions I asked the staff at the two hotels where we had stayed previously, by the searches made in the streets that he knew, and finally, in the car with the nuns and their driver, by visits to the hospitals, the mortuary, even the airport. Because the police will not intervene until a person has been missing for twenty-four hours.

Finally, it was actually the police, the tourist police, who picked up Francesco on the third day, to my indescribable relief. They had found him at Rosetta, one of the two large cities on the Nile delta, 70 kilometres from Alexandria. He had been seen by the police as he wandered around in a state of bewilderment, and was taken to the police station where, thanks to his passport, he was recognized as a tourist and where he must have spent most of the time. The police drove him back from Rosetta to Alexandria, where I went to collect him from another police station.

'But *how* did you find me?' Francesco exclaimed, amazed but ecstatic when he saw me arrive, a phrase I was to hear many times in the following months. I couldn't find words to reply, being too distraught by his gauntness, the bruises that covered his arms, his broken watch, his bleeding toenails that bore witness, all too clearly, to the ill-treatment he had experienced.

At the old people's home, the doctor, who examined him very carefully and asked him several questions, took me aside while Francesco was dressing. 'Your husband is sick and I suspect it may be Alzheimer's'. He then described the symptoms of the illness and the disorders and characteristic behaviour I should expect. For the first time this word entered my world, bringing with it the drastic upheaval of our life.

A HOST OF complications marked the rest of our stay. The first night after his return I saw Francesco burst into my room a little after midnight, fully dressed.

'I'm going back home', he declared. It took a long time to persuade him to undress, to explain to him that we were travelling, to reassure him. He was in a state of great agitation. The following day I asked for my bed to be moved into his room and I prepared myself to fulfil my new role of guardian, a role that from then onwards I was never to relinquish.

We stayed a further ten days in Egypt, it being the time needed to clear my mother's apartment and arrange the sale of her furniture. During this time Francesco had moments of lucidity and was able to advise us and value the authenticity of some pieces of furniture and objects with all his previous accuracy. But most of the time I noticed with increasing consternation his repetition of irrational acts and his disorientation. He spoke very little of the incident and his days in Rosetta, and was unable to explain how he had got there. From his first account, I deduced that he had lived with a group of prisoners with whom he went in the evening to a place with 'long benches' where they were served a 'ghastly soup', while the 'bosses' enjoyed their meal comfortably seated at tables. He told of being made to do 'heavy gardening' and I presumed that he had probably tried to weed the garden at the police station. But soon these memories disappeared.

This incident will always remain for me as a dark and unfinished chapter to which I often return, even today, with deep distress. I still imagine Francesco wandering along strange and hostile streets, unable to understand or to make himself understood, and in my frequent nightmares the scenario of his disappearance and of my desperate search is always the same.

Finally the time for our departure arrived. The train between Alexandria and Cairo runs alongside the canal that at one time linked the Nile to the sea. The scenes that we know from paintings and bas-reliefs of the Pharaonic ages are still the same: the *fellahin* in light striped *galabeyas* still till their fields with the archaic hand tools of that time, day and night the buffaloes, blindfolded and with their slow and ponderous tread, still turn the axis of the *sakheyas* that groan plaintively while emptying the water buckets into the irrigation canals. But all around, like an oil stain, extend the new neighbourhoods, fruit of the recent industrialization, real shanty towns which hold the suburbs of Alexandria with a vice of misery.

Our friend Mohamed had come to pick us up at the station in Cairo. Francesco did not recognize him and the evening passed with considerable awkwardness, despite the dinner offered us by our host at the Piazza restaurant which, apart from classic Italian food, also serves exquisite Egyptian dishes. Francesco ate absentmindedly; I noted with anxiety the growing uncertainty of his gestures, the fork that did not always reach his mouth, the food that fell off the plate. I dreaded the night and the risk of another escape. I dreaded the plane journey, which already on our way to Alexandria had been the cause of great distress. In fact, Francesco never stopped describing the almost vertical ascent of the Boeing on take-off. He kept illustrating with this hands the way the plane had shot up into the air, and I wondered how much his deterioration had been due to those moments of terror.

The following morning the plane was leaving at seven and we had to be at the customs before six. Francesco kept asking anxiously 'Will they make me wear a uniform? Will I have to pilot the plane?' I explained that we were only passengers, trying, as I never ceased doing, to reassure him…

Unfortunately, during our stop-over at Athens there was a loudspeaker message announcing a two-hour delay for our flight to Rome. 'Watch your luggage. Beware of pickpockets', threatening signs repeated everywhere. I had gathered our cases around us. But Francesco was again very restless, he wanted to get up, walk around, he was thirsty; I kept my eye on him while I went to buy him a drink but I was not able to stop him going off in the direction of the airfield. The hostess at the gate sent him back but he was determined and insisted he wanted to pass through and a brief scuffle ensued in which I had to intervene, leaving our luggage unattended.

Our return to Rome, although a relief in many ways, was just the beginning of a series of incidents that confirmed the diagnosis made by the doctor in Alexandria.

Chapter Six

I had signed a translation contract with FAO, the Food and Agriculture Organization of the United Nations, which I could not cancel, partly because there was no time to find a substitute and partly because I thought that back in Rome, in familiar surroundings, Francesco would improve and I would regain a little independence. Instead of which, they were nightmare days. Sometimes I took Francesco with me to the office and entrusted him to the security guards, seating him with books and magazines in the hall where I went down every hour to check the situation. Other times he stayed at home, looked after by Irene.

Francesco insisted on continuing to drive and I did not know how to stop him without offending or humiliating him. He often forgot where he had parked the car, partly because, due to his pressing need to keep on the move, he kept moving it. One day when I had left him at home with Irene and was feeling relatively relaxed, I received a telephone call in my office from a colleague. Francesco was wandering around the FAO restaurant looking for me. I was aghast. I dashed up the eight floors that lead to the restaurant, ignoring the lift and its slow stops, and found my husband firmly restrained by two friends: he was so pleased to see me that I didn't feel I could remonstrate with him and we had lunch as if nothing were wrong. 'And the car?' I asked him afterwards, 'where have you left it?' 'I don't remember...', and so once again our desperate chase began around the parking places near FAO.

Soon my contract ended, but it was clear that from then on I would not be able to accept any work that took me away from home.

I THINK GREAT risks were taken during those first days that were the most difficult for me to cope with and where I found myself without even the slightest help. Today I still ask myself how I could have left Francesco to wander around the streets of Rome on his own, how was it that I did not understand the dangers? I now think that perhaps a sense of fatality was born in me, as though the accumulation of uncontrollable events had annulled my capacity or will to react. Or perhaps I thought that by pretending that all was normal I could bring normality back.

THE ALEXANDRIAN EPISODE was the start of a new sequence of events in which Francesco, who had always loved being in charge, deciding and taking initiatives, leaned increasingly on me. However, there were still many lucid moments in which he was able to act autonomously, to make decisions without hesitation, following an apparent logic, but interspersed with an ever increasing number of confused periods.

He remembered, for example, that when we bought the apartment in which we were living, he had wanted the contract to be in my name, but as he no longer recognized me, he planned meetings with our lawyer to change the terms. In vain I showed him my passport to convince him that I was still his wife. 'Nothing more simple than changing a passport photograph', he declared obstinately, looking at mine and not recognizing me in the photo.

My constant presence kept in check more serious or dangerous episodes and lessened risks of the unexpected. To avoid the repetition of Francesco's trying to use the car and to prevent him leaving the house without my knowing, I hid his driving licence and the car keys. Despite this, finding the car locked one day, and with clear reasoning, he went to our mechanic who runs a garage opposite our house and requested his help. The good Vincenzo, unaware of what was happening, did as he was asked while I watched from the window with dismay as they inserted a piece of wire through the car window and tried to pull up the opening catch.

It was only when he lifted his head and saw me, that Vincenzo, correctly interpreting my gestures, persuaded Francesco to abandon his plan.

THESE EPISODES WERE very painful for me. It was difficult to take certain decisions without wounding his dignity and each one of my interventions was preceded by a thousand hesitations. I still tried with words and reasoning to bring Francesco back to logic and often I was prey to impatience and irritation. But in my desire to save our normality at all costs there was still, even though fainter and fainter, a glimmer of hope.

THE TIMES WHEN Francesco did not recognize me and believed I wished to cheat him occurred more and more often. I remember that one day, while I was driving him home, he insisted that I take him to FAO where he usually came to meet me after work. 'I promised I'd go and collect her, I always do, I must keep to the appointment', he insisted. My assurances that this person was, in fact, seated at his side did not convince him at all. 'I must go, it is already late', he insisted. And so, to avoid useless arguments, I accompanied him to the FAO entrance where I waited for more than half an hour while he walked up and down outside the gate.

At home the situation was completely reversed. 'You know', he said indignantly, 'there was a horrible woman in the car who wanted to stop me from coming to collect you... If she ever comes here I swear I'll throw her out.'

EVEN IF DURING the day I managed in some way or other to control the situation, the night revealed the true dimension of my helplessness. Francesco never slept. Many times I was awakened by the smell of gas and one night, uneasy at his absence, I found him sitting at the kitchen table ready to eat a meal consisting of dried lentils seasoned with hot paprika and a glass of vinegar poured over it.

On the rare occasions when I managed to close my eyes I found, on awakening, that the house had been turned into a battlefield: drawers opened and their contents scattered around, clothes spread all over the room, papers strewn everywhere. Other times he passed the whole night wrapped in his overcoat, sitting on guard at the window watching the road. Often he prepared food to soothe the police who he was afraid were going to come for him: large bowls of pasta seasoned with tomato sauce were lined up every evening in front of our door. At that time he also went around armed, with his pockets full of scissors and knives.

Everything was wrapped up: shoes, ornaments, books. In every corner of the house mountains of parcels rose which I quickly unpacked when I managed to direct his attention elsewhere. At night, madness reigned. While I was utterly exhausted, he was full of an uncontrollable energy, never showing any sign of weariness, and at dawn he was still absorbed in his activities.

To reduce the intensity of this phenomenon, our doctor prescribed some tranquillizers which, for most of the time, had no effect whatsoever. There was no way he would agree to submit to more specialized examinations. 'Do you think I'm crazy?' he cried. I knew then that help would have to be sought elsewhere.

Chapter Seven

My brother Jean, a retired doctor, lived in Caen in France, together with his wife Marianne and their married daughters. Jean usually gave me good advice, as did Benoît, his son-in-law, an excellent psychiatrist who was already well established despite his young age. It seemed to be an ideal place to ask for assistance. Also at Caen it would be easier to convince Francesco to undergo the examinations he refused in Rome. The visit to France was organized as a holiday and Francesco, in a lucid moment, was delighted at the idea of the trip.

It was obvious, but I still did not know it, that the change of scene would make things worse. In fact, as soon as we arrived at Caen, he went into a state of uncontrollable excitability and total incoherence. Furthermore, remembering the familiar gestures of his trade, he spent his days moving furniture around in the sitting-room. My relatives were deeply concerned.

The medical examinations, which I pretended had been prescribed for me and to which he submitted 'to keep me company', revealed extended brain atrophy. No doctor had mentioned Alzheimer's but by now, more expert, I recognized the symptoms predicted by the doctor in Alexandria. Among these, what had struck me most was his drastic loss of memory. In fact, all his computer expertise acquired in the months preceding his disappearance had vanished on our return from Egypt. Francesco did not know even how to turn on the computer, let alone how to find his programs and files.

ALTHOUGH THE FRENCH doctors did not give any clear pronouncements on Francesco's illness, they were in agreement that he should return to Rome as soon as possible, especially after the signs of disorientation and violence that appeared a few days after our arrival.

One evening after dark, Francesco had left the house unknown to us and was found wandering around the streets. When he saw my brother at the corner of the road, he was frightened and with all his strength pushed a huge rubbish bin towards him, missing him only by a miracle.

Seeing my relations as dangerous spies he tried to protect us both from their sinister plots. 'Be careful of that woman', he whispered, while we were going out with Marianne in the car to do the shopping, 'she wants to hurt us, she'll try to kill us.' On other occasions, instead, I was the spy...

FOLLOWING THESE DAYS of great restlessness and aware of my distress, Jean advised me to admit Francesco into one of the Caen hospitals. 'To carry out other examinations, to recover your equilibrium and to enable you to sleep a bit', he said to me, to overcome my resistance. And so it was done.

One morning we called an ambulance and Francesco, under the effects of a powerful sedative, was taken away on a stretcher. I didn't dare look him in the eyes – I felt his departure as my betrayal.

In the calm and normality of Jean's house, I began to ask myself questions and wonder about the future. The more I analysed the situation the more I felt overcome by panic. What attitude should I adopt? How does one cope with dementia? Who would help me? Francesco had neither children nor close relatives in Rome. His cousins were all older than he. Furthermore I had no knowledge of the help provided by the State to assist mentally ill patients nor the procedures needed in order to benefit from them. I knew nothing of the immediate steps that should be taken, faced now by a situation that had suddenly become explosive. It seemed that the treatment consisted of administering neuroleptics but I had also seen that they often had no effect, leaving Francesco at times even more restless.

And so, in the absence of an acceptable solution, I began to plan our return. I booked two berths on the sleeper for Rome and, dreading another escape, begged a friend to come and collect us by car at the station.

But in Paris, at the Gâre de Lyon, a bitter surprise awaited us. Due to a forty-eight-hour strike, all departures had been cancelled, and because of this it was practically impossible to find a hotel. Before returning to Caen, and after endless telephone calls, Marianne managed to book us a room into which I promptly locked ourselves. That evening, while Francesco was undressing, I noticed he was wearing an incontinence pad. So incontinence had begun again and a new problem was added to those already known. Meanwhile, Francesco, standing in front of the door, was violently shaking the handle trying to escape. I remember the efforts and words of persuasion that were needed to induce him to go to bed. I spent the whole night awake, mentally going over all possible solutions, and also the financial implications.

The next day I managed to find two tickets for the Air France flight leaving for Rome. But at the airport, there were new problems; Francesco refused to board the plane. 'I can't leave without my father, he is waiting for me over there', he insisted, indicating the waiting-room and forgetting that his father had died more than thirty years earlier. It was useless to reason, by now I understood, and assuring him that his father was following us I grabbed him by the arm and dragged him with all my strength towards the plane entrance, under the anxious eyes of the flight attendants. Fortunately no one reacted and the departure took place normally. I hate flying as much as Francesco, but that day I prayed that the plane would come down, thus putting an end to my torment.

SOON REASON TOOK over from panic and I began to make concrete plans again. First, I had to get Francesco to take up his Italian residency which he had lost when we left for Canada and not bothered to take up again. It was the only way that he could be eligible for the benefits available to people in his condition. Then I had to find a good specialist properly able to assess his case and give me valid advice. But most important of all I had to recover my own sanity, shattered by the ordeals of the past weeks.

Chapter Eight

As soon as we got back to Rome I spared no time in seeking the necessary documents. Residency could be obtained without too much delay. Francesco meekly accepted signing all the papers, and obediently answered the Registrar's questions as though he had suddenly surrendered to my newly acquired authority. He was also much calmer since we had returned home. I continued to administer the sedatives prescribed by the French doctors but had not yet resorted to psychiatric help. He slept a lot now and longer, and I had to make great efforts when he was drowsy to rouse him from the sofa and lead him to the dining-room, bathroom or bed. When he slept, his sleep was so deep that he became a dead weight and I had to resign myself to waiting sometimes for hours until he awoke. I tried to reduce moving him as much as I could, and if he fell during the night I limited myself to covering him with a blanket and placing a cushion under his head. The following morning I then asked my neighbours for help. However, sleep often alternated with moments of great recalcitrance and, when contradicted, he sometimes reacted violently, hurling things at me or smashing the crockery.

THE PSYCHIATRIST WHOM I eventually consulted did not change the treatment prescribed in Caen but only advised adjusting, a drop at a time, the dose of sedatives, depending on Francesco's reactions.

Deprived as I was of any form of assistance with Francesco, and by now feeling somewhat afraid and discouraged, I had to admit that the situation had deteriorated and that I was no longer able to cope on my own. With the help of the same psychiatrist, a period of hospitalization was arranged for Francesco in the psychiatric ward of San Giacomo Hospital.

WHILE I PREPARED Francesco's suitcase, a friend, familiar with hospital ways, had recommended 'Don't pack too many things, you won't find any of Francesco's belongings when he leaves the hospital.' Saddened, I took out a few clothes from the suitcase and called an ambulance. I tried to convince myself that this was a positive step in the right direction: the hospital doctors would assess the disease, prescribe a treatment, give me useful guidelines. Meanwhile I would have had time to think and take the necessary decisions.

The paramedics arrived while Francesco was dozing on the sofa, but he woke up at the sound of the bell and, remembering a past experience, he addressed the two young men in French. I could not hold back my tears. He, instead, calm and trusting, lay down on the stretcher.

The ambulance left us at the hospital and Francesco, now sound asleep, was undressed and put to bed. 'I'll talk to the senior consultant in the morning', I said to myself. The only thing I wanted now was to get away: my second betrayal had just taken place.

I FOUND MYSELF in the middle of the via del Corso, on my arm Francesco's coat, which the nurse had returned to me saying that he would not need it. I remember that I was so upset that I did not recognize the normally familiar surroundings, nor the street that stretched ahead, nor the shops with all their lights still on, nor the square I caught a glimpse of in the distance. I could have been in a totally unknown city.

That night I was unable to sleep in our bed or sit in the kitchen, too full of memories of the evenings we spent together cooking, inventing new recipes or trying to remember some exotic dish we had eaten during our trips. While I was drinking a glass of wine and preparing a sandwich I gathered my thoughts and started to plan our future. It was obvious that Francesco could not stay long at San Giacomo Hospital. But after? Each long-term solution involving hospitalization seemed to me unacceptable but for the moment I saw no alternative.

Not much time was given me to ponder, because early the next morning the senior consultant was on the line, insisting that I went to collect Francesco. He was not, as it had seemed, a psychiatric patient but an organic one, and therefore this was not the appropriate place for him to be. Furthermore, Francesco on awakening had shown signs of great restlessness and had suffered new episodes of incontinence, antagonizing the nurses who were eager to get rid of him. I rushed to the hospital and helped him to dress; I collected his few remaining belongings: as had been forecast his wallet, pullover, socks and other articles were missing.

FOLLOWING ANOTHER CONSULTATION with our psychiatrist, we selected a new clinic. The place was more welcoming and acceptable than the hospital, and Francesco was given a pleasantly furnished room with two beds that he was to share with a young patient.

He spent a few days in that clinic where I went to visit him regularly and where his disorientation increased progressively, even though he obediently submitted himself to the rules of the house. But my peace and quiet were short-lived.

One day, summoned to the clinic by the senior consultant, I heard him state once again that Francesco was not a psychiatric patient but an organic one and that I was to take him away within the next two days. There were more consultations with my psychiatrist, but there was no time to take any decision because, the very next morning, the senior consultant phoned me to announce that Francesco had been transferred without further ado to another clinic whose name was totally unknown to me. Using the scant information I managed to collect as to its whereabouts, I drove there immediately and arrived as Francesco was alighting from the ambulance in a state of total confusion, anxiety and terror. When he saw me arrive, the same words with which he had greeted me after his return to Alexandria came to his lips: 'But *how* did you find me...?'

FRANCESCO REMAINED IN that clinic for two and a half months. He was neither happy nor unhappy, but often prey to great restlessness, reflected in his pacing up and down the endless corridors of the clinic and in actions that sorely tested the patience of the nurses and assistants. I was asked to devote part of the day to him, otherwise a personal nurse would be needed. Naturally, I preferred to remain by his side.

Often I found him in his room restrained in an armchair that was in turn tied to the radiator to prevent him dragging it around the room, as he was a strong and determined man. I felt deeply humiliated for him and as soon as I arrived at the clinic, the first thing I did was to free him. Then I helped him put on his coat and together we went down into the garden for a breath of air and a walk. Seated on a bench, he holding my hand in his pocket, we would look towards the mountains, across the railway and beyond the industrial area, to the little valley where Gallicano and our house nestled. I talked a lot to him about the house and about the time when we would go back and see it, hoping to create some beacons in the increasing fog that now enveloped his brain. He did not react or talk much, only wanting to walk. On our return to his room he would fill a glass with water and put in it the cuttings that he never forgot to gather.

I tried also to stimulate his pleasure in drawing by bringing him paper and pens together with photos of our journeys, hoping they would remind him of our adventures, and I invited him to reproduce those photos on the paper. I also bought puzzles to do together until, one day, mistaking the pieces for sweets, he tried to eat them. We then turned to dominoes and also cards, which he once enjoyed but now they did not seem to arouse him. The one thing I could rejoice in was that he seemed insensitive to the groans and cries emanating from the neighbouring rooms.

And the same time, day and night, I was filled with an overwhelming feeling of guilt. I spent sleepless nights and drugged myself with tranquillizers to escape from my own thoughts and from the depression into which I was sinking ever more deeply. When asked where he was, Francesco limited himself to answering very simply 'on board', expressing his old dream of keeping on the move, his rejection of permanent ties and his thirst for adventure. Instead, there he was, in that clinic, restrained in an armchair that was tied to a radiator. I could not imagine anything more degrading.

It was then that I took the decision, come what may, to take Francesco home.

Chapter Nine

'Don't do it. It's too risky, its better to leave Francesco where he is', exhorted my friends. 'You won't be able to cope with the situation on your own. Sooner or later you will have to bring him back', warned the clinic director, giving me also to understand that conditions could be less favourable the next time. But by now my decision was firmly made and nothing would have induced me to go back on it.

With the help of friends and acquaintances, I looked among the groups of immigrants in search of jobs for a suitable candidate to employ as an assistant. The candidate obviously had to be male, reliable and willing to live in, available and, above all, have a pleasant personality, because I had no idea how Francesco would react to the intrusion of a perfect stranger into our close life as a couple. Then one day I met a young man from Sri Lanka whose gentle ways and dazzling smile immediately won me over. He did not ask too many questions and I was loath to describe the gravity of the situation lest he took fright. He was available, ready to start and accepted my conditions. And that is how Laki became part of our life, staying with us for more than three years. I decided to call him 'Lucky' in an attempt to challenge fate.

Of course I knew very well that Francesco's return would turn the apartment upside down. The dining-room became Lucky's bedroom and room had to be found in the cupboards for his personal belongings while a dining area was squeezed into our living-room. But nothing mattered to me: I had to have Francesco home again.

Lucky arrived early one morning at the beginning of March, loaded with packages and dragging a large suitcase tied together with string. I felt at peace, more certain than ever that I had made the right decision and, for the first time in months, I was happy. Obviously, I had to calculate the possibility that Francesco might have violent reactions or that Lucky might get discouraged by his behaviour. But I preferred not to give in to such useless speculation.

I gave Lucky Francesco's suitcase and we set off to the clinic.

WHILE I WENT through the last administrative procedures and the doctor was preparing the case history, Lucky had already folded all the clothes and placed them tidily in the suitcase, while Francesco, wearing his green loden coat and dark red cashmere scarf, my last birthday present, around his neck, was calmly waiting in his armchair.

We got into the car, Lucky behind and Francesco sitting next to me. From the corner of my eye I could see his profile sharpened by the illness, his face now inexpressive but on which I could also read an infinite and absolute trust, as though he had now surrendered his whole life to my care. I was overwhelmed with a sense of pride and a surge of enormous strength. 'We'll make it', I said to myself. No more wavering and indecision, no more remorse or shame. Francesco and I had lived through many an adventure and this would not be the last.

It's done! We are at home. Francesco looks around, curious, pleased. After an absence of two months, he has completely forgotten the apartment. He does not recognize it as his but it seems that he likes what he sees. He potters around, touches the furniture, the ornaments, sits down at his usual place on the left of the sofa, admires the large bookcase made by him. He observes the panelled walls of the large living-room that he himself designed. 'This is beautiful', he whispers, and I melt with tenderness.

DESPITE MY JOY at having Francesco home again, I feared the repercussions of his return. Afraid that after the strict discipline of the clinic he might be upset by the more relaxed rhythm of family life, from the very beginning I set down exacting standards. First and foremost I was worried that he might have a negative reaction towards Lucky who, despite his smile and limitless goodwill, represented an extraneous element, a sudden intrusion into our intimacy. But I had not taken into account a factor that was to radically change things and dispel my fears. Francesco remembered absolutely nothing of his previous life. His past had literally been erased and was now replaced by his present reality. Sometimes I remained incredulous at the depth of this oblivion and I attempted to bring back his memory in the way one tries to stir a sleeping person. I tried to re-establish the communion we had once had when it was enough for one of us to think of something for the other one to say it. I attempted to penetrate the mist that now blotted out his thoughts and to read into them, to bridge the rift that now separated us so painfully. But I also had to invent new programmes, new routines to fill in this blank space that stretched ahead. I think that Lucky and I 're-invented' Francesco's life.

ONE OF MY daily tasks that caused me most worry was the preparation of our meals. At first I had feared that I would have to dedicate far too much time out of my already crammed day to satisfy the dietary needs of three different people. I had not yet asked Lucky what his eating habits and preferences were nor investigated his cooking capabilities. Happily the problem was solved almost immediately in that Lucky was fond of Italian cooking, in particular pasta with tomato sauce, which he admitted he could prepare 'a bit'. I had filled the store cupboards with all kinds of rice, believing it to be an Asian boy's staple food. But Lucky loved pasta and cooked himself hefty portions of spaghetti every day. Having watched me make an omelette one day, the next time he took the eggs himself, tapped them delicately all around one by one with a fork and then broke them with a firm hand into a plate. 'So you know how to cook!' I exclaimed. Visibly satisfied, he gave me one of his beaming smiles and revealed that his sister, who worked as a cook with an Italian family, had taught him the basics of our cuisine.

I also feared Francesco's displeasure at feeling expelled from the kitchen that he considered his realm. He had an inexhaustible inventiveness in that field and nothing could make him happier than replacing me at the cooker if I was busy, or in concocting complicated dishes to sample with our friends. But now, even though he had not lost his pleasure in food, the way in which the dishes were cooked barely interested him. Trying to imitate the diet he had become used to in the clinic, where the dishes were very varied – at home we were always battling against cholesterol and weight problems – I had inaugurated a tasty menu with the food he liked and later encouraged Lucky to take on full responsibility for the preparation of the meals. And indeed, this arrangement was well suited to his patience and his pleasure in slicing the vegetables and mincing the meat so finely that in the end it was almost impossible to distinguish one from the other when cooked. In time Lucky became an excellent cook and I ended up by delegating the preparation of our meals entirely to him.

BESIDES THE COOKING, we also had to establish a strict timetable for Francesco's medical care. When we left the clinic, the senior consultant gave me a list of medicines to administer at regular intervals and in very precise dosages. However, a few days after Francesco's return, we had to drastically reduce the prescribed dosage. Almost immediately he had entered into a state of lethargy out of which nothing could draw him. He slept continuously, and often at table his head would keel over the plate or he would forget to swallow the food that he kept in his mouth for hours. The dosage of sedatives had to be halved and then halved again. We then had to stop them altogether, while Francesco went on sleeping day and night, as though he were trying to make up for his lack of sleep in the previous months. This situation lasted several weeks. I was convinced that this profound lethargy was due less to a saturation of sedatives than to the reassuring and calming effect of being at home. All this helped to confirm the soundness of my decision.

AS TIME WENT by, there was a gradual resumption, but on a much lower scale, of Francesco's former restlessness. Another problem also soon arose, that of incontinence. Initially, when he was accompanied to the bathroom, Francesco managed quite well on his own, and following the doctor's advice, I had tried to prolong his autonomy and delay as much as possible having to use incontinence pads. 'Let him do everything he can still do; each forgotten act is lost forever', the neurologist had said. For a long time we tried to follow these rules, but when the situation deteriorated further I had to resign myself to this inevitable and unpleasant reality.

Every concession made to the illness tasted of a failure. Francesco, still with a very strong sense of modesty, asked my forgiveness each time I changed him.

NIGHTS WERE PARTICULARLY difficult. Lucky needed to get as much sleep as he could in order to be able to cope with the daily chores. Therefore night was my personal responsibility. For a long time we continued to share our double bed. When Francesco grew restless in the early hours of the morning we talked. I tried to answer his questions in my usual way, and because of the improved blood circulation in the brain when he was lying down, these were often quite reasonable. Sometimes he would go back to sleep, but most of the time he wanted to get up and roam around the apartment. Initially this was the source of many security problems. Before his return from the clinic I had installed a security device in the kitchen against possible gas leaks, as well as another one for electricity. I had checked all the doors and made sure they locked well, then removed the keys. The kitchen was locked when not in use and the key always taken away. The bathroom key was placed in a hidden corner. Nevertheless, one day Francesco found it and locked himself in. Despite our instructions and explanations, there was no way we could make him understand which way he had to turn the key, and in the end I had to call in a carpenter to take off the door. After that, Lucky and I each kept our own bunch of keys. I felt as though I had become a prison warder.

SOMEONE HAD MENTIONED the Italian Association for Alzheimer's Disease and one day I decided to go to Sant'Eugenio

m and had to
's sudden and
g of the gums
ves publicised
ch I devoutly
nd falling out.
d their disap-
hosen hiding
ad discovered
his socks and
e found them
flower vases.
laboratory not
uld and adapt
r, the problem
diate measures.
to leave the
ures became a
one day at a
who offered to
ng and anxious
ed up with her
kitchen where
s, as necessary.
metimes refus-
was his inalien-
hich the work
and strenuous,
e tension, Sofia
of persuasion to
to leave, instead
ion, he took the

Hospital where, in co-operation with that association, support group meetings were organized monthly for the families of patients. Thus one Thursday afternoon, I found myself sitting in a large room given over for our use by the hospital. There were many of us that day too, I remember, and each person had a story to tell of suffering, desperation and helplessness. Listening to them I felt deeply disturbed and afraid. I was still in the initial phase where there is a refusal to believe that the illness truly exists, and hope for an improvement is still strong, where one tries to ignore a future that can lead to worse, bearing in mind the present difficulties. As with so many of the others I too was reluctant to ask about the various phases of the illness, fearing to lose a courage already very shaken and refusing to face in advance the slow but inexorable end awaiting those suffering from Alzheimer's. Certainly it was a serious mistake on my part because I was depriving myself of a lot of help and support. I remember that I practically fled before the end of the meeting, my heart beating wildly. On my return home, because I was so tired and upset, I forgot to lock the front door after me.

That night I went to sleep on the living-room sofa to make sure I would get a few hours' sleep, but I could find no respite. Around two in the morning, a familiar sound made me jump to my feet: the subtle but unmistakable click of the front door closing. I ran to the bedroom, but as I had anticipated, found it empty. I pulled on my dressing gown and reached for my slippers and I was in the street. I looked around frantically but could see no one to the right or the left. I felt I was reliving the dramatic days in Alexandria. To the left of our building runs a narrow sloping street. I took this and at the bottom of the slope found Francesco, fully dressed, wearing his green coat and corduroy cap, striding out purposefully. I ran down

and reached him: 'Francesco. Wait
cried. 'Home', he answered, withou

THE LIFESTYLE WE had managed
identifying clear benchmarks and
opportunity to make the most of th
had. I thought, for example, about
never wanted in the apartment, cc
means of information only able to
particularly fond of television mys
more objective and dispassionate i
space for the imagination. The arro
often the indecency of many tel
always bothered me. But now th
seemed to me that television migh
and variety to our day. And so I fac
new, of finding a suitable set of a s
too much in our house. To my utmo
not opposed.

After dinner, Lucky would join
together we watched programmes
Naturally he was fond of football
spent many an evening watching
ships. There were also interesting
countries which provoked longing
he recognized landscapes from
Francesco observed all this with v
some impatience. Sometimes he a
dialogued with the actors, but for th
towards this device that took my
and he would stand in front of the
looking at it.

Now we were in charge of this delicate pro
monitor carefully their whereabouts. France
marked loss of weight had produced a shrin
and, although we sampled the strongest adh
on the television and sold on the market –
took note of – the dentures kept coming loos
Annoyed, Francesco usually took them out
pearance was a nightmare for us. In fact th
places changed constantly, even though w
that his favourites were the drawer containi
the kitchen cutlery drawer. But other times
under the cushions of the sofa or even in th

Two young dental technicians, who ran
far from the apartment, took it in turns to
them according to the circumstances. Howe
soon arose again and we had to take more imn

When Francesco was no longer ab
apartment, the question of adjusting his d
drama without any apparent solution un
friend's home I met Sofia, a dental technicia
come to the apartment. Sofia was patient, wi
to help Francesco. She came to our house lo
instruments and installed her laboratory in t
she filed, remoulded and corrected the dentu

Francesco vigorously opposed all this,
ing to open his mouth, justly deeming that
able right to keep it closed. One day in
carried out had been particularly delicat
leaving both Lucky and me exhausted from
had used all her technical means and power
get Francesco to co-operate. As she was abou
of presenting her with his usual sulky expre
young woman's hand and kissed it.

'TONIGHT I REALLY need to sleep…' Sleep had become a persistent preoccupation for me. I never managed to rest enough. Despite the sleeping pills prescribed by our neurologist, Roberta, by now our faithful counsellor, Francesco slept very little at night. Often, after having checked that all dangers had been eliminated, I would go and sleep on the sofa in the living-room, the door of which could be locked. Sometimes, Francesco would get up and sit behind the door, waiting for me to wake up. I still was unable to rest in peace. One night he fell and hit his head against the radiator. I had to wake Lucky to help me get him back to bed. Usually, after an hour or two, rather than remaining awake and listening to every sound, always fearing the thud of a falling body, I would go back to the bedroom and lie down beside him.

I had learned to steal an hour of sleep here and there and to make rest coincide with his, and even to sleep a little between our various dialogues, because Francesco chatted a lot during the night. He asked, as he used to in the past, 'And for today, what are our plans?' or 'What are we going to do now?' He always spoke of *us*. This absolute dependency had set in gradually. In the beginning I found this irritating and tried to divert his persistent concentration from me. I was even abrupt with him at times. But then I understood that I had become his only pillar of strength, his last rock, and that inspired in me a great desire to help him. He had given over his whole life to me and I felt joy and tenderness in offering him my support. I would then take his hand, that hand now so emaciated, the skin so transparent that with my finger I could trace the blue network of his veins, and I would hold it tightly in mine.

Chapter Ten

I sought by every means to try to anchor Francesco's mind to real, solid things, to all that had been our life together, to that past that for me was still alive and was part of my present but for him had now vanished. I tried to revive his memories, to live again with him the experiences that had deeply marked our existence and tried anything that would help me reach that aim. One day I thought about our photographs.

We had taken masses of photos during the years in which we worked as photographers for the United Nations, and although a large part of them were in the hands of the agencies who sold them on, we still had a great number at home. I thought I might use them to arouse his interest, take him back to a time when he was alive, enthusiastic, carried away by his ardent need for adventure, in short, the time when we made our long journeys. I had a special box of slides of a rather large size that could easily be seen when held up to the light. There were also hundreds of photographs in black and white. And so, with these photos I tried to recall with him the most important phases of our trips, the moments that were engraved most deeply in our memories. For instance, on many occasions, I used the pictures taken during our first trip to the Sahara.

I showed Francesco the photos one by one, describing to him the various stages of our journey.

HERE WE ARE in Nefta, in Tunisia, at the edge of the Great Oriental Erg, the vast desert of dunes that links Southern Tunisia to Algeria. Our road, which crosses through part of it, will soon become a track, the Hoggar track that runs through the Sahara from North to South and will take us, beyond the Sahel, into Niger. This is one of our first journeys in North Africa and the pictures show us during one of our stopovers in the midst of the dunes, marvelling at these huge mounds of sand in which we sink up to our knees. Here is Francesco, ready to assault a dune, hair falling over his eyes, camera hanging from his neck, a hand over the lenses to protect them from the sand, the other pointing a light-metre to the ground. I dwell for a while on this picture and would like to help him relive all the emotions of those very first Saharan days, our almost reverent silence facing this vast expanse in which the apparent stillness is in reality pure movement. The dunes, like scythes, seem to be sculpted in marble, while a silent wind in perpetual motion models and moulds them, changing their direction, honing the ridge till it is as sharp as a knife, and digging deep grooves on the windward face. Here we are, enraptured, initially reluctant to violate this pure design, this shimmering coat, then unable to resist any longer the temptation of becoming part of it, of taking possession of these images, we launch ourselves forward, our feet leaving deep pits in the sand, similar to the tracks of elephants.

Francesco held the photos a little longer between his fingers. I did not know whether he had recognized himself in them but he was smiling.

OTHER PHOTOS ILLUSTRATE our itinerary towards the south, from the stony Tademait plateau to the plain of In Salah, where more than once the sand hampered our progress. Then the passage through the gorge of the Arak Wadi with its strangely polished black rocks, the grottoes harbouring ancient rock engravings, to the Hoggar massif, the deeply indented silhouette of which rises unexpectedly in the midst of the vast sand plain, and finally Tamanrasset, one of our most important targets, the capital of the realm of the Tuaregs.

Our new acquaintances, travellers with the most diverse nationalities and aspirations, coming from all parts of the world to sample the mystery and the magic of the desert appear in our photos. Here is Robert with his friends wearing Tuareg garb arrived from Morocco in a large zebra-striped bus that we met shortly before reaching Tamanrasset. An immediate friendship was established, as is the rule when fellow travellers meet in the absolute isolation of the desert. There is the blue Ford Transit tightly packed with Scandinavian girls on their way to South Africa, who never lost the chance to slip into their bikinis and sunbathe as though they were on the beach, apparently indifferent to the dangers in store for them on the sandy tracks of the Sahel. And finally Eric and Tom, two young Englishmen heading for Nairobi in a tiny 'deux-chevaux' but who, for the time being, seemed quite terrified by the adventure they had launched into, and were wondering how they made it so far in their rickety Citroën. They were to be our companions for the rest of the journey as we could not ignore their appeals for help and deny them the shelter of our large camper.

I showed Francesco the beautiful shady street bordered with feathery tamarisks that runs through the city. Along this street, in small groups, with their little fingers playfully locked, and to the sound of loud high-pitched laughter, the Tuaregs stroll in their multicoloured robes, endlessly winding and unwinding their interminable turbans, as though to punctuate their conversation.

I FELT THAT Francesco showed most interest in the second stage of our journey, the Sahel, that Southern shore of the Sahara where, after the desert crossing, imperceptibly, almost miraculously, the first tiny silver blades appear, a fragile down at first, then the thicker grass and the long creeping stalks of the colocynths, the small desert melons, and finally the endless grey ocean of the acacias. Starting from stunted thorny shrubs bearing bunches of small fragrant yellow balls, they grow progressively taller as the Sahara recedes.

AT TIMBOULAGA WE had our first meeting with the local nomad herdsmen. Men with dark complexions gleaming with glints of copper in short leather tunics, their faces hidden by pointed straw hats embellished with metal discs, and tall women, walking bare breasted with majestic gait, hips wrapped in a loosely woven light blue fabric, ears pierced by the seven traditional ear-rings which, according to the wealth of the tribe, are of silver or gold. These are the Mboro, the herdsmen who dominate these plains, leading their gigantic herds of zebus with lyre-shaped horns.

Attracted by the shouts of the herdsmen and the lowing of their cattle, we penetrated into the huge cloud of dust that hovered over the well where the watering was taking place. The wells were few and scattered throughout the Sahel so that every watering session turned into an occasion for a festive ritual. On the mouth of the well the nomads had built a rough structure of crossed branches to which four wooden pulleys had been attached. Through the pulleys ran four ropes the end of each being fastened to the collar of a white camel. At a given signal, the camels walked away, led by four women, pulling out of the well the enormous goatskin brimming with water that was then tilted by the men into a watering-trough.

It was like being a bystander to an ancient rite the chore-ography for which had been set once and for all, a thousand times repeated and never changed, and where each gesture evoked a millenary design.

That day Francesco, exhilarated, took photos all the after-noon, oblivious to the dust, the water spray, the threatening horns, establishing with his enthusiasm a friendly and playful dialogue with these herdsmen, their fierce faces marked by deep scars and carrying bows and poison-tipped arrows on their shoulders.

'Do you remember, Francesco, I was afraid of those arrows but you were not worried at all, and joked with the herdsmen who wanted you to test the tips!' I said now, trying to jog his memory.

Reliving those unforgettable moments, I tried to channel his attention, to trigger off a reminiscence, pointing with my finger to the most important scenes.

As TIME WENT on, Francesco's falls became so frequent that I was forced to resort to a solution I had delayed as much as possible: putting in a hospital bed. It was yet another defeat that added itself to the now long list of my failures and provoked a deep sense of discouragement in me. When the bed arrived, I tried to explain its purpose to Francesco, but he initially rejected it strongly. 'How awful!' he said each night, entering into the bedroom.

And thus a fresh upheaval took place: our bed was elimi-nated to make room for this cumbersome object equipped with bars. Next to it I had set up a folding bed for myself, so as not to leave him alone during the first nights. In the end, I slept in this bed for all the remaining years of Francesco's illness.

At first he struggled vigorously against the bars, like a freedom-loving man forced to sleep in a cage. He pushed with all his strength against the bottom of the bed and sometimes tried to slip through the bars, often remaining trapped. I suffered intensely, and tried to calm him down. After a while he got used to his bed and our nights became peaceful once more.

WE OFTEN WENT to Gallicano for the day, especially during the summer to water the plants and in autumn to prune them. Francesco no longer came very willingly. Once out of the car he looked around, bewildered. I made him sit in the armchair facing the window from which he could see the silhouette of the little town perched on top of the high rocky hill and surrounded by trees, a sight that had once been a source of great enthusiasm. Sometimes he said 'This is the most beautiful place in the world', transfixed by the view that had awakened forgotten emotions in him, but he soon tired and after strolling a little with me through the house, arm in arm to prevent a possible fall, he would go back to the car that had now become his refuge. Later I used to go to Gallicano alone, and when Francesco's memory had totally gone and he was unable to suffer the loss, I sold the house.

Chapter Eleven

Sunday was different from other days. Dressed in his best clothes, Lucky used to leave home early in the morning to return late at night, leaving me on my own with Francesco. I tried my best so that the day would be special for us too, and planned drives to places that might still mean something to Francesco and bring back memories. Knowing how much he enjoyed looking at beautiful houses, noble palaces, squares and monuments, I was able to take him right to the centre of town as traffic is allowed to circulate on Sundays. He loved to go to Piazza Farnese where he could still appreciate the splendid lines and the grace of the sixteenth-century palace and he gestured in admiration towards the two handsome fountains that decorate the square. These signs of recognition renewed my hopes.

Many times we walked from there to Piazza della Cancelleria for a glimpse of our favourite restaurant and to look into the windows of the shop that used to supply us with photographic material. I pointed to the cameras displayed in the windows reminding him of their names. 'Here's the Nikkormat I used for colour slides', I said to him, and 'See, there's an old Leica similar to yours'. He looked obediently into the windows but seldom uttered a word.

Another of our goals was Villa Borghese and the Lake Garden, for which he always had a soft spot. There we would sit and eat a sandwich at lunch time, observing the great white swans glide over the lake or the turtles emerge in silent formations. But Francesco could not remain seated for very long, urged on by an irresistible and constant need to move. He tired easily and as soon as we returned to the car he would fall asleep. However when, on our way back, we reached the point where our route crosses the street in which stands his childhood home, he would wake up with a start: 'This is where you should have turned. You are going the wrong way. Our house is there...', and he got very distressed as we continued on our usual way. After that, I had to change our homeward route.

I LIKED TO take Francesco for walks along the narrow streets of our neighbourhood. Our apartment is in an area surrounded by gardens in the old hill district of Monte Sacro. It had been our habit, in the past, to wander around in search of new unknown areas in the labyrinth of streets that wind their way along the gentle rises of the hill. Often the street ended in steps that led to different levels offering new vistas and unexpected glimpses of luxuriant gardens that had bestowed the name of Garden City to our neighbourhood. Francesco always returned from our walks with bunches of cuttings for our garden, already bristling with a great diversity of species. We knew all the Latin names of these plants and when one or the other particularly caught our fancy, we would go and hunt them down in the garden centres in Rome.

I kept that habit for a long time, taking Francesco twice a day to the places that he had been fond of in the past. I showed him the plants, one by one, naming them as we went along so that he could remember their names. In particular, close to our house there was a deciduous magnolia, *Magnolia soulangeana*, which in spring was covered by a mantle of mauve flowers in the form of tulips. Francesco loved that tree and watched its development daily, just as he did with certain climbing roses called 'Cocktail', with a deep pink corolla and at the bottom a ring of white, that we had planted in Gallicano to decorate our gate.

Another of our destinations was a tiny penthouse at the top of an old villa, whose bright yellow terrace overlooked the Roman hills. Two palm trees guarded the entrance to the villa. 'How I would love to own it', Francesco always said as the sun-kissed terrace came into view among the trees. 'It really is a dream house.' I said nothing, but thinking back to the many dream houses Francesco had designed, especially the one in Canada and another in London, both the source of a raft of problems – not to mention the house in Gallicano – I wondered whether we really needed another! But for Francesco houses were his raw material. He designed them for others as though for himself. All those where we had lived together had been planned with such loving care that all the daily needs of a housewife were catered for. However, as soon as one project was finished, he immediately started another, so that we never remained very long in the same place.

I WANTED HIM to store all these images in his memory. But, as the months went by, I noticed that he raised his head less often to follow my pointed finger. And so, for as long as we could continue our strolls, our dialogue became a monologue, while Francesco walked silently, with small shuffling steps, his hand tightly clutching my arm.

In the fading light of those winter afternoons, our lengthened shadows fell over the pavement. He, so tall, although now a little bent, and I, proud, guiding him. This familiar image often comes back to me in my memories of that time.

Chapter Twelve

A mong the questions that played an important part in my decisions for our future were administrative ones. Francesco owned the house in Gallicano and also had other properties. Now he was no longer able to administer these and the responsibility fell entirely to me, although I was not authorized to act in his place.

The problem was extremely serious and impeded many of my initiatives, especially when the question of selling Gallicano arose. We seldom went there now and maintenance was difficult and costly. What I needed was to have general power of attorney.

The notary I approached clearly gave me to understand that such a document would only be valid if the signatory was sound of mind, fully cognizant and able to make decisions. It was obvious that Francesco did not meet any of these requirements.

Furthermore, I noticed with growing concern that his ability to write, let alone to sign his name, had dwindled dramatically. In the days prior to our meeting with the notary I made him practise his signature many times over. The result was mostly unreadable scribbles, although sometimes he managed to write properly formed letters with a certain ease. However, in the end it was always a matter of chance so that one could only hope for a propitious day.

On the day of the signature, the notary – the son of friends – who had promised to turn a blind eye on any strange behaviour by Francesco and not dwell on the more sensitive clauses of the deed, came to the clinic. He took out a double sheet of a legal document with all its four sides filled in from his briefcase and I saw with dismay that, despite his promises, he was about to read them all out in full.

I dreaded Francesco's reaction, remembering his annoyance on 'finding out' that our apartment was in my name, and his deep diffidence towards me in those moments when he did not recognize me.

The reading seemed endless, and the text, like most legal documents, was incomprehensible because of excess details. Francesco listened, at times carefully and at times absently, even when the notary underlined certain points that explicitly set out the transfer of all rights to me.

I was on tenterhooks.

In the end, Francesco was asked whether he approved the contents of the different clauses, as well as agreeing to the decisions made, and he, with a clear voice, answered 'If it's all right with my wife it's all right with me', and with a firm hand he took the pen and signed the document. Such miracles were rare and entirely unexpected.

OFTEN TWO OR more public holidays took place before or after a Sunday so that sometimes Francesco and I remained alone for several days. It was hard to find diversions to fill in all this time. But another problem arose. Because of the neuroleptics he was taking, Francesco had begun to suffer from 'extrapyramidal' problems during which he lost his vertical balance, so that when walking he tended to lean backwards. Several times I had found myself in the middle of the street when this phenomenon occurred and had to grab him firmly by the shoulders and push him forward with all my strength. This is why our Sunday outings were reduced to a minimum, and then suspended.

Not only was it practically impossible to find help during those days without Lucky, but I also lived in great fear of Francesco's falling, so that in the end we always used to stay in. I dreaded the approach of Christmas, New Year, Easter, Ferragosto (Feast of the Assumption of the Virgin Mary) and other holidays.

One Sunday, while he was roaming around the house, Francesco tripped over an armchair. His fall was inevitable. I was powerless and absolutely unable to pull him up. Furthermore, our neighbours upon whose help I knew I could usually rely were out for the day. While I was trying to think of what to do next, the door bell rang. On the threshold stood two ladies, Jehovah's Witnesses, their arms filled with literature about their activities and anxious to save my soul. I welcomed them warmly and, after we had got Francesco back on his feet, I tried to show some interest in their preaching. The Jehovah's Witnesses included me in the circle of their followers and often on a Sunday they would come to visit me.

Later it became essential to find regular help on Sundays and other holidays. This is how Deepal came to join our family, while I lost another few precious square metres of my already curtailed area of privacy.

Francesco was always fond of classical music. He played the piano rather well and had a great passion for Brahms, Mozart and Beethoven. After his return home from the clinic, I often played music by these composers. I watched him, for instance, as he listened attentively to Brahms' Fourth Symphony, which always moved him in a special way. He sat on the sofa concentrating on the poignant melodies of the first tempo where the theme leaps from one instrument to another in an unending and aching search for resolution. He would sit there, roused by the arrogant and impetuous entry of the orchestra and relaxing, after the storm, when the theme resurfaces triumphantly, free and pure. He liked the great virtuosity of Mozart's piano concertos, so clear, limpid and balanced, especially the pensive melancholy of certain andantes and the seraphic tenderness of the adagios. He listened with his head slightly bent to the sudden modulations, the unexpected passages from major to minor that never fail to produce that sudden skip of the heart.

Together we had listened so often to these pieces, falling in love with the crystalline sweetness of the melodies, enclosed but never trapped in the rigorous structure of the classical form. But Francesco's favourite piece by far was Beethoven's Seventh Symphony, where the triumphant and stirring notes of that hymn to joy exorcise the dark tragedy underlying all his other symphonies. Francesco was never tired of listening to it, and once he gaily whistled the theme along with the orchestra.

I personally had a special affinity for the tender impatience and the delicate intimacy of Schubert's impromptus and his malicious, flirtatious but always elusive dialoguing.

Now I presented all these works to him again, but a little at a time, so as not to put too much pressure on his now diminished concentration. In fact, any object at hand was enough to draw his attention away from the music. But I insisted because I firmly believed in the therapeutic power of that form of art.

SUNDAY AGAIN. A long afternoon stretched ahead, with bad weather preventing us from going out. I also knew that Deepal would be coming late. Having leafed through a couple of magazines, I brought out the photos once again as this seemed to me the only way to keep Francesco quiet for a while. I asked him if he wanted to see some more, and he agreed, perhaps mostly out of curiosity, even though he followed the movements of my hands attentively.

HERE WE ARE in Mali, a country where we had spent long periods of time and that we loved more than any other. I pored over the photos taken in the great central delta of the Niger river which, in the twelfth century, had been the seat of the Mali Empire, and in the city of Mopti, at the entrance to the delta. Here every week a great fish market takes place where all the ethnic groups of the area meet: Songhais and Somonos, the dominant races, but also Peuls, Bambaras, Toucouleurs and even Dogons, come down from the Bandiagara cliff.

Our arrival coincided with market day and we were already there at dawn, just at the moment that pirogues and other boats brimming with fish were coming in from every corner of the delta. In the river harbour, which opens like a huge shell on the southern bank of the river and gently slopes towards the water, women were already waiting, seated inside their canopied beach-chairs, ready to buy the goods they would later sell at the market, making friendly conversation but ready to turn into ferocious competitors. In a short while the harbour of Mopti was teeming with thousands of boats that came in without pause from all directions. We had been told that in moments when affluence was at its peak, more than twenty thousand people could be gathered in the harbour.

However, our job was not to photograph the market but a fish canning plant where a United Nations expert had taught the local fishermen new conservation techniques.

Unfortunately, his mission completed, the expert had left Mopti and the plant had been closed.

I showed Francesco the pictures of the plant. Not at all disconcerted by this setback, he had simply asked the Malian superintendent: 'Will you open it for us. We want to take our photos just the same!'

A little worried, the superintendent returned to his office in town and came back holding a large rusty key that he inserted with some difficulty into the lock; the door creaked on its hinges. 'You know, it has been closed for so long.' The stench of rotten fish still permeated the air.

'Now we will need a few actors', said Francesco who had in mind a very well-defined plan, and no pity for the poor superintendent who was watching this incursion with growing concern. It did not take us long to get a group of volunteers together from among the fishermen, who agreed with good will to don the white coats of the trainees. 'And now for the fish', insisted Francesco. 'Where from?' asked the superintendent with increasing alarm. Francesco made a broad gesture towards the harbour 'From there'.

In the harbour, the gondola-shaped pirogues were now squeezed in tight rows and crammed with fishermen, their nets still glistening from their last hauls, and tradesmen in their garishly coloured traditional *boubous*. Tons of fish were piled on the beach in various forms: live, just unloaded from the nets or already smoked or dried in the villages. The predominant element, the fish filled every corner of the harbour. It was handled by the women, who first smelled it, made their selection of the best and threw the rest back into the pirogues, and by the children who gleaned those fallen from the nets. And Francesco, with his usual irony, remarked 'I don't think it will be difficult to get hold of some fish!'

'Do you remember? The training programme did not envisage having to buy fish and now here we were forced to purchase a few kilograms of catfish to make the scene more realistic!'

That evening a big party had been organized in the village with people coming from the whole delta. Thanks to the intervention of the superintendent of the fish-canning plant, now our friend, we too had been invited. It would have been a wonderful chance to take some very special photos, but despite my plans and the flashes I had ready, I took no pictures that night. In fact, while I was still loading my camera, I was suddenly swept to the dance floor by a Tuareg warrior, complete with sword and dagger, an amused look filtering through the folds of his indigo veil, and before I knew it I was swirling around in his arms while he tried to teach me the complex steps of the traditional dances.

SOMETIMES FRANCESCO WOULD dwell on a particular picture, and his eyes would suddenly light up as he listened with curiosity to my stories. This was all the encouragement I needed.

Chapter Thirteen

One day, without any warning, Lucky told me that he would be leaving. He was going back to Sri Lanka where his wife was expecting a baby (how he ever managed to get her pregnant was a mystery, whichever way one looked at it) and that he was booked on a flight for Colombo the following week. I was distraught by this news and ever more aware of the precariousness of the ménage that I had so painstakingly created. Francesco was very attached to Lucky and had put all his trust in him. Now the fragile equilibrium of our family life was about to collapse. Where would I find at such short notice another helper as reliable and caring as he?

THE FOLLOWING DAYS proved very difficult. Francesco immediately showed stubborn hostility towards Lucky's first successor, Kamal, who had none of Lucky's patience and gentleness. One day Kamal carelessly let Francesco slip in the bathtub. This young man did not remain long and was followed by various others who stayed only for brief periods. I was starting to lose all hope of getting our life back on a normal track when one day Darshana came to the door. Tall, with an intelligent face, this young man had a natural and almost awe-inspiring elegance and I pondered for a quite a while on the wisdom of recruiting him. I wondered for how long he would accept the humble and often unpleasant tasks that were in store for him. In the end he won me over.

From the very beginning, and despite his distinguished appearance, Darshana never hesitated to undertake all the chores, even the most burdensome. I was also soon reassured as to his cooking skills as he immediately declared that he could make an excellent tomato sauce, no doubt part of the early training these young people receive when they come to Italy. Francesco liked Darshana from the start and they were soon on friendly terms, installing the same relationship of deep trust that had existed between him and Lucky. This was apparent in the mornings when he was under the shower: while with Kamal complaints, shouts and insults were heard in the bathroom, now with Darshana all was quiet and Francesco appeared for breakfast clean, well shaven and with a change of clothes every morning. Order and routine had been restored: meals were served at regular hours and Francesco had recovered his serenity.

Three years had gone by...

ONE MORNING WE noticed a sudden deterioration in Francesco's already laboured walking; his right leg had become stiff and now he dragged it, unable to lift it anymore. Our walks together had ceased as I feared not being able to get him home safely, even though I always carried my mobile telephone with me. Furthermore, when one day I was trying to help him walk up the stairs I strained my back and for several days I was unable to move around. It was a warning. I could in no way risk an accident: my presence was needed all day and every day. I therefore had to delegate many of my functions to Darshana.

When walking now, Francesco kept his eyes glued to the ground and seldom looked around, except when he passed in front of the cars parked along our street. Then he would stop, examining them one by one with a sudden interest. 'Do you want a new car?' joked Darshana. 'Which one of these do you want to buy?' and each time Francesco smiled in response.

When he had started to go out with Darshana, I often used to meet him on my way home from shopping or from work. Darshana would then say 'Look, look, Madam is here', and he would lift his eyes and fix his gaze on me at first without recognizing me, but then, when recognition returned, his face would light with a joy so intense that I was always deeply moved.

FRANCESCO HAD ALWAYS been strongly interested in the technical side of any activities he undertook and was extremely competent in solving problems that for me were well-nigh impossible. 'It's useless, I haven't got a technical mind', I used to say to justify my ignorance. But for him such hurdles only represented challenges. He used to attack problems head-on and drew immense satisfaction in solving them. I did not take any part in those triumphs, preferring to leave such expertise to members of the opposite sex. With Francesco that strategy did not work. He was convinced that with some thought and logic anyone, be it man or woman, was capable of overcoming all difficulties. 'It's just mental laziness', he used to reply to my protests. Humiliated, though having to admit it was often true, I had gradually become familiar with the tools he used. And so, as time went on, I learned to use the screwdriver, the pincers, the pliers, the trowel, how to prepare a good creamy cement as well as to putty, sand and finish wood cabinets, to paint whole rooms including the ceiling, to restore furniture, and to upholster chairs and armchairs. Francesco was a very accomplished but demanding task master.

In spite of all, I had been unable to understand one of his last logical actions. One evening my computer had suddenly broken down. It was brand new and I was still unfamiliar with many of its features. An hour earlier it had been working perfectly with the screen illuminated, then, for no apparent reason and without any warning, the screen went blank. I had an appointment that evening and I left the house in great anxiety because I had been unable to finish an urgent translation.

The following day, as the problem had not been solved, I called on my technician who quickly found that Francesco, probably bothered by the glare of the screen, had turned the little gadget that regulated the intensity of the light until the screen blanked out.

These unexpected logical reactions, appearing like sudden flashes from a brain in progressive and visible regression, took me by surprise. A similar episode occurred one day when I was driving Francesco to the Lake Garden. I had parked the car alongside the laurel hedge bordering the ramp leading to the parking area but I had not left enough space on my side of the car to get out. I helped Francesco to get out first, then followed, locking the left door as I did so and then the right one from the inside, but leaving the keys on the seat. Just as I was about to slam the door, Francesco sensing the danger immediately grabbed my arm. 'The keys!' he exclaimed, pointing his finger towards the seat. 'Otherwise we won't be able to get in again…'

ROBERTA, OUR NEUROLOGIST, had prescribed a series of physiotherapy sessions to help loosen Francesco's joints, strengthen his muscles and improve his walking. And so it was that Cristina came to our apartment. She was a good-looking young woman with a gentle expression, slim and fair, just the sort of girl that Francesco admired, and in fact he was immediately attracted. I was pleased at this and I saw him ready to co-operate, noticing the beginnings of a pleasant relationship, of new opportunities for him to collaborate with another type of person; I also rejoiced in Cristina's youth, and looked forward to her livening up the monotony of our daily life. I introduced her to Francesco as a friend who was coming to keep us company and presented the physiotherapy as a game for the three of us to play. Hence, I looked with optimism and trust to the introduction of this new element into our family nucleus. Instead, my expectations were very quickly dashed. Francesco soon got bored and firmly refused to carry out even the simplest exercises. I had rented a walker which he began to use unwillingly. During one session, he had tried to climb over it instead of pushing it. We tried to play ball, but when the ball fell to the ground Francesco refused to pick it up.

After having left them alone at home one day, on my return I found the young woman very angry. 'Your husband insulted me', she said, offended. 'I'm not coming back here again.' I found out later that, in a moment of unexpected lucidity, he had told her to 'Go to hell!' and tried to throw her out of the apartment. Not always with positive results, in moments of extreme tension he was never at a loss to express his feelings while our everyday conversation was now reduced to a few essential phrases. I was sorry that Cristina, whose dynamism and efforts to encourage Francesco's physical activities had been so promising, had decided to leave and it was with great regret that I had to close the chapter on physiotherapy. It seemed that Francesco, suddenly shrewd, refused to be taken in by false promises and had unexpectedly identified the truth.

ANOTHER CHRISTMAS LOOMED ahead. Whatever their religion, Sri Lankans always celebrate the Christian feasts of Christmas and Easter. Darshana, for example, was particularly pious and always asked to be allowed out in the afternoon to go to mass. I found his devotion laudable and on his birthday he stayed for a long while in our neighbourhood Church of the Guardian Angels. It was only after a long time, and through a careless slip of his tongue, that I learned that he was in fact a Buddhist and that his outings had never included going to church.

That particular Christmas was starting badly. The public holidays were three days in all and I needed to plan long ahead to avoid the endless pacing around the apartment and the risk of falls. There was yet another problem to face: the disappearance of many items in daily use, especially the books I was reading, my pens and pencils, and dictionaries. The pens and pencils were usually to be found in the pockets of Francesco's jacket or his dressing-gown, but searching for the books was more complicated although, later, I found out that they were usually hidden under the mattress or the sofa cushions. Other things the disappearance of which I did not immediately notice risked vanishing for good, such as the sixty-page manuscript of the translation of an important and urgent report. Not yet an expert on the computer, I had typed it out laboriously and this was never found.

Trying to fill in these three long unending days I resorted again to our magic box of photographs. With many words of encouragement and some persuasion I managed to convince Francesco to sit next to me, and together we sorted through our inexhaustible archives of photographs.

This next group of pictures I chose shows us about to leave Mali; a treacherous stretch of sandy desert separates us from Gao, our next stopover. The road, we were told, crossed kilometres of *tôle ondulée*, as the French-speaking Africans call this as yet unexplained phenomenon that transforms the sand into a sort of corrugated surface which, at a certain speed, shakes the car with such violent jerks that the wheel is no longer controllable. We were not ready to face this ordeal and looked for an alternative.

The advice from the Tourist Office was to join the convoy of barges that was used to transport goods on the river. There was one leaving just that day and we hurried off to contact the captain. 'No problem', he assured us with optimism. Yet there was a problem: how to board the barge now rocking violently against the quay. 'You just need a thick plank or a sheet of metal', he advised, as though such items were to be found in any corner of the harbour. However, luck was on our side, and at the market we came across the exact type of plank that would serve our purpose. Having bought some supplies, because the trip would last from two to three weeks, we were ready to embark. And this is how the most fascinating stage of our journey in Mali began.

Although we had requested and paid for a barge for our own exclusive use, shortly before departure, a local woman came on board followed by a goat. It was useless to protest and we had to resign ourselves to sharing our already limited space with these cumbersome companions. The goat was soon tied to the wheel of our camper, while the woman, pious Muslim as she was, unrolled her prayer mat in front of our door. The goat's plaintive bleating accompanied us for the rest of our journey.

With our camper firmly anchored and our travelling companions settled in, our barge glided over the turgid waters of the Niger, or rather the Joliba, as the river is known locally, meaning the great river.

Thanks partly to the photos and partly to my stories, Francesco remained serene that afternoon. I made him repeat the names of the places shown in the pictures. Mopti was easy to pronounce but not Niafounké or Timbuktu, where we arrived one day after a week's navigation, excited at the prospect of visiting this mysterious city, the goal of so many travellers of the past.

The convoy stopped at each village to deliver and embark goods, mostly sugar and cases of tea from China. Up to their waists in the water, the Peul women were aggressively selling the milk contained in their huge floating calabashes, a traditional activity of their tribe, while other vendors brandished live chickens held up by their legs or proffered bowls of rice or eggs. These exchanges were vigorous and the negotiations brisk because whole families of fishermen lived on the barges, and the women spent most of their days cooking. The aromas wafting from their covered barges held the promise of tasty dishes and they floated in the evening breeze over to our camper where, with our small gas stove, we were able to produce little more than a vegetable soup or pasta with canned tomato sauce.

We spent the day on the roof of our camper, shielded from the blinding sun by the two enormous leather-trimmed straw hats that we had bought from the Dogon merchants at the market in Mopti.

'Look Francesco, this is you!' I exclaimed, but he did not recognize himself in that outfit and just smiled at my enthusiasm.

In the evening, when the mist shrouded the villages and the last shepherds deserted the pastures of the delta, herds of hippopotamuses appeared. A quivering mass, they entered the water with a ponderous tread and rolled around in the warm mud, their huge mouths yawning, watching us pass at a respectable distance.

After Timbuktu, by now given over to mass tourism, which was for us a searing disappointment, the delta ends and the river resumes its normal course in a narrowing bed. The landscape changes abruptly, the green pastures give way to desert while the river banks rise in two tall escarpments on each side.

We had lost all sense of time because Francesco, before leaving, had put our watches into a drawer. 'They won't be needed', he had declared. We had lived in this fluid temporal space for almost three weeks when, one morning at dawn, the convoy sailed into the waters of the Gao harbour, our final destination.

Chapter Fourteen

The large writing-desk in the corner of our living-room was a source of irresistible fascination for Francesco. He stared at it every morning, seated on the sofa at the other side of the room until, unable to wait another minute, he would go over and sit in front of it. This writing-desk spoke to him, reminded him of his adolescence, but above all of his moments of activity and creativity. He had designed new houses here, planned our garden in Gallicano, even written his first poems when just a boy. He had tried to write poems at the beginning of his illness, as though his mind had taken a sudden leap back into the past. He wrote about Rome, for instance, although he harboured a love/hate relationship with our capital city. He said that Rome, which he had once loved, where he had lived in tiny penthouses with terraces always bigger than the living area, had disappointed him, betrayed him: it had become the megalopolis that it is today with its devastating effects on human relationships.

Now, however, in his new state, it seemed that Rome had once again acquired its former fascination. In one of his recent poems he had written: 'Rome is our destiny. Life all around it is splendid, so that it will strive to...?' But the words ended there.

Francesco had dedicated many efforts to Rome in the past. In the renovation work on houses the windows were always designed to frame a special view: a picturesque old roof with moss-covered tiles, a belfry tower, the moulding jutting from a Roman cornice, the luxuriant foliage on a neighbouring terrace. In one of his penthouses, he had filled the central room with plants, and then taken off the roof, transforming it into a patio.

Francesco had an intimate knowledge of every corner of Rome. Shortly after we had met, we often used to wander around the deserted streets in the historic centre and take pictures. An abandoned chair, lit by the dim light of a street lamp, throwing its long shadow on the gleaming pavement; a broken-down scooter leaning against a wall; an old bottom-less rocking chair; a rag-and-bone man's cart chained to a gate, all took on mysterious appearances and meanings.

He normally sat very straight facing his desk, opening the drawers decisively then rummaging in them for a long while, searching for something that he was unable to remember or to identify. At times, old habits resurfaced and he would light an imaginary cigarette and draw sensual puffs of smoke. Then he would tap with his forefinger that invisible butt as though to knock off the ash. At other times he would lift a virtual cup of coffee to his lips. Often he turned round towards the shelf with the gardening books and chose one. I would then go and sit beside him and together we would leaf through books the pages of which were full of notes and drawings and from which he had derived ideas for the garden in Gallicano.

But after a while his attention dwindled and his need to pace up and down took over.

On Sunday evenings, at the beginning of Francesco's illness, we often went to dinner at Annalisa's, a very dear friend of ours who never seemed taken aback by Francesco's often unpredictable behaviour. To dine on the small terrace of her penthouse in via Sardegna, overflowing with plants which one had to brush firmly aside to enter, had always been a joy. I had to start the long procedure entailed in dressing Francesco in the afternoon. He was fussy about his clothes. Once he had donned his favourite dark red sweater and pulled on his blue velvet trousers, or in the summer his blue batiste shirt with the white dots, he would stand for a long time in front of the mirror, adjusting the collar of his sweater or his shirt, and running his fingers through his hair to tidy it.

Despite such long and elaborate preparations, the evening was usually over in a flash. In fact, before we had even finished our drinks, Francesco would take his seat at table, thinking that he was in a restaurant, and at the end of the meal he used to jump to his feet and impatiently pace the floor.

We tried to delay leaving, prolonging the evening as much as we could by asking him questions and then suggesting the answers, but in the end his restiveness won and we had to return home.

The return journey was never easy because of Francesco's difficulty in getting in and out of the car, and I was often worried about being alone with him at night in our deserted street. He never understood that to get out he had to put out one foot first, but remained seated, his legs pressed tightly together, his feet firmly planted. When I managed to pull out one of his feet he immediately put it back. 'Francesco, pull out your foot', I insisted, but he simply stared at me, not understanding. One evening we risked spending the whole night in the car because of his total refusal to co-operate. In the end, and because, unawares, I had used words that he probably recognized, he finally put one foot on the ground and I was able to get him out. After that I dared not go out with him alone by car when I was on my own, and later I had to give up our outings altogether. For me it was a day of deep sadness because it marked a new step along the backward road that was now ours.

I HAVE OFTEN wondered if Francesco, at that stage of his illness, was not perhaps a fantasy figure resulting from my efforts to give him an identity, and if, unawares, I had created an individual who was no longer Francesco but an invention of mine that I had superimposed on his true personality. These thoughts worried me deeply, although I knew that all my initiatives were aimed only at helping him to cope better with his dementia. He no longer had the instruments to fight, or the means to contradict or communicate his desires. I wondered whether or not, unconsciously taking advantage of his weakness, I had cancelled out important traits of his personality. In other words, had I tried to mould him into a person who would fit in with my convenience?

Could it not be that dementia has a logic of its own, different from ours, but perhaps just as valid? In trying to put him back on the right track, did I not risk breaking the fragile equilibrium of a demented man? Too often I had to recognize a very precise form of coherence in his behaviour. Sometimes I began to think that rationality is a little like faith. Who holds the truth? Why should I be so convinced that my logic was the best?

A few months after Darshana had come to live with us, I started to worry about the time that had elapsed since he had applied for a residence permit. He had the receipt for his request, a slip of paper that he had proudly shown me to ensure that I would take him on. Since then nothing more had materialized despite the repeated calls at the police station made on his behalf by his uncle. I decided I had to intervene.

One morning, carrying a photocopy of the receipt in my bag, I went to the police station and explained the case to the inspector on duty. He closely scrutinized the slip of paper then disappeared into another office where he consulted with a colleague at length. On his return he announced: 'I want to see this young man, tell him to come here with his passport.' When I got home I recounted all this to Darshana who seemed deeply upset. He told me that his uncle had his passport but he did not know when they would be able to meet up. A little concerned I pressed him. Then the truth came out. A few months after arriving in Italy, some of his countrymen had sold him this receipt for a substantial sum of money. It was only later that he realized that the document had been forged, but he had not dared tell me.

The news was shattering. Without knowing I had employed an illegal immigrant, convinced that he would soon have his papers in order. To legitimize his situation he would have to return to his home country, while I made an official request to employ him and the Italian consulate in Colombo rubber-stamped it. Months could elapse before he would be allowed to return. However, it was essential to act quickly, particularly in view of the recently approved very strict immigration laws giving rise to huge fines on those employing illegal immigrants. So Darshana's return home was organized, while I looked around for a replacement.

Prey to panic, I spent many a sleepless night remembering the difficult days experienced after Lucky's departure. Several young men came to the house, all with various attributes of good will and intelligence, but it seemed impossible to find the right person, spoiled as I was by the good manners and competence of Darshana. One of the candidates who had seemed to be best suited left us after barely twelve hours, on the pretext that a skin allergy prevented him from washing Francesco. Another, despite his assurances that he was used to housework, spent the morning moving the furniture around and then forgetting where to put it back again.

One evening, after I had interviewed a series of applicants – all accompanied by friends and relations so that it was sometimes impossible to distinguish between the applicant and his escort – and I had finally closed the door on the last group, Francesco, distraught, fell trembling into my arms, like a big terrified child. I knew then that I had no other choice than to ignore rules and regulations and get Darshana back. Now aware of being irreplaceable, he immediately asked for a substantial rise in salary.

Chapter Fifteen

Francesco had been experiencing speech problems for some time. The painful and often vain search for the correct word that had characterized the first years of his illness and that had caused such frustration, because the word chosen seldom corresponded to his thoughts, tended now to disappear. Even the words were confused and the sounds he emitted resembled only vaguely the words sought. Initially, when he used the wrong word, I laughed with him as though the mistakes were part of a joke, and together we would try to find the correct one. Later, he seemed to have resigned himself to being unable to say what he thought. He no longer understood very well what I was saying, although I endeavoured to use easy phrases, avoiding complicated reasoning, expressing very simple concepts like 'Let's go to the table', 'Let's go to the bathroom' or, at night, 'Let's go to bed', a suggestion that always triggered off some protest. In fact he was no longer in a position to recall the experiences of the past. Now I had become his memory.

Despite these increasing limitations, we lived in peace. Our ship was steady. Francesco's aggressiveness and violence had vanished and we were able to progressively diminish and later completely abolish the neuroleptics. Francesco only took one sleeping pill at night to sleep – and thus allow us to sleep also. I knew that Alzheimer's is a disease with a slow evolution, that the patient can live for many years provided physical functions are not impaired. I was ready to accept that situation and tried to derive from it the most positive aspects. I had long overcome those distressing moments where one refuses to accept reality, where one tries to attribute dementia to a normal process of ageing and where one hopes that things will improve. I knew perfectly well my hopes were futile, but my only desire was that the sickness would not develop too quickly and that it would leave us a little more time to love each other and to express it mutually. I had learned to control my impatience faced with the irrationalities and the obsessive repetition of certain acts that sometimes almost seemed to touch on provocation, and to overcome the irritation roused by Francesco's behaviour – like the telephone left unhooked, the unwashed plates put back into the kitchen cupboards, the lights left on all night, the disappearance of important documents: in brief the lapses that are sadly common to all Alzheimer patients.

'MADAM, THE FURNITURE in your house is dangerous. All these sharp corners will have to be padded otherwise you will need to change it. This house in not suitable for someone as sick as your husband.' Such was the peremptory declaration of a neurologist specialized in the treatment of Alzheimer patients, whom I had called upon during an absence of Roberta. After the neurologist had left, I looked around, disconcerted. How could I implement this recommendation? Get rid of all the loved objects we had brought back from Canada on our return to Rome? Pad all the corners! How and with what material? Before me rose the vision of our furniture padded with foam-rubber. I knew for a certainty that Francesco would immediately try to rip off the padding as soon as he saw it. It was also true that he spent much of the day wandering around the house sometimes with great precariousness. Squeezing, for instance, through the narrow space between my legs and a coffee table, or between two armchairs. It was true that he had always liked to move the furniture around. On more than one occasion, I had to stop him from lugging heavy chests of drawers across the living-room – a clear reminder of his past activities as an interior decorator. But I did not want to suppress these initiatives, signs of a remaining vitality. Even when his walking had become hesitant and unstable, he had always managed to thread his way through the hurdles of the apartment without hurting himself. So I ignored the alarmist neurologist's advice and the furniture remained as it was, giving Francesco the comfort of its reassuring presence.

In fact, the furniture provided landmarks for him. One of these was the big English barometer that towered above our entrance and where he was used to checking the daily changes in climate, and that he still now observed attentively. Then there was the halt in front of the large portrait of his mother, to which he always seemed to want to pay homage. Francesco had never wanted to introduce me to this domineering woman, fearing negative reactions on her part. In any event, she died a long time before our marriage. I knew she had a brilliant mind but also that she was pathologically possessive. Francesco loved her as much as he feared her. I think that his continuous desire to keep on the move, his love of travel, his need to constantly change houses were all due to his wish to escape from her. But now that she was no longer there and no longer to be feared, Francesco had wanted to conserve her memory with the huge portrait that hung from the wall of our living-room. The painter had portrayed her in a Renaissance attitude. She sat majestically at the centre of the picture with, at her back, a series of arches framing glimpses of a Tuscan landscape. The stern expression on her face was belied by the relaxed posture of her hands with their long, tapered fingers, gently folded on her lap. But the look in her eyes was perturbing and disquieting.

Finally he paid tribute to the three wooden African statues, three women in a hieratic position, their angular faces dominated by voluminous geometrical hair arrangements, and their bosoms jutting – a sign of fertility – that occupied a niche in our library. In the folds of the skirt of one there was still some dust from the ground millet used for ritual offerings. Francesco was extremely fond of these statues, also because they spoke to him of his travels, his Africa, his times of greater vitality. He never passed by them without stopping, caressing their austere profiles devoid of any expression, their hands lifted in a gesture of invocation.

All this was Francesco's present world and nothing could ever have induced me to change it. I knew its dangers but I trusted in fate, whether good or bad, as well as my intuition, and I have never since had reason to regret it.

WE WERE WELL known in our neighbourhood. The shopkeepers, whose windows faced onto our street, witnessed our daily activities. No doubt there was some nosiness there, something to gossip about later, but also, and I think above all, there was compassion and a desire to help when the need arose.

When, for one reason or another, I went into one of these shops, the owner always expressed an opinion: 'Your husband is looking better today' and 'He seemed a little tired, this morning, but what can you expect with all this rain…' Other times: 'It's been a long time since we have seen him', when bronchitis nailed Francesco in bed for several days. And so it was that, through their comments, I too was able to follow the progress of the disease.

Their generosity was touching. Bruno, the manager of the bar next door, reminded me of his willingness to help when I passed in front of his shop. He knew about Francesco's frequent falls. 'Just call on me, Madam, I'll help you to get him back on his feet.' And it was the same for Renato, the plumber who had a workshop almost in front of our door: 'And how are we doing today...?' Anna who ran a dry-cleaning shop had more than once helped me get Francesco back home when he suffered a loss of equilibrium. Carlo, our grocer for many years, personally made deliveries on the days when I was alone with Francesco.

Therefore, I knew that I could rely on neighbourhood support even though, deep inside, I felt a certain reluctance to let outsiders witness our hardships and I tried to protect Francesco from a curiosity that at times was a little invasive though always well meant.

One of the places most regularly frequented was the barber shop, where Darshana took Francesco to have his hair trimmed and, at the same time, to have his own hair done as well. At first I was amazed at the frequency of such visits, which did not always correspond with the length of Francesco's hair; but then I realized that it was Darshana who was more in need of the barber than Francesco, as his thick head of hair required constant attention.

As time passed and Francesco's state of health worsened, these friendly comments became rarer and I understood that the shopkeepers had noticed his gradual deterioration, the increased stoop of his shoulders, his ever more fragile appearance.

GREAT HARMONY REIGNED between us. Francesco would hold his eyes to mine and his gaze followed my every movement. As soon as I tried to get up from the sofa, he held me back with amazing strength, as though he feared I might disappear. Many times he tried to dress himself in my clothes, often the coat or jacket I had left on an armchair. He was strongly attracted by bright colours and more than once I had seen him donning my red raincoat, a favourite of his. 'It's beautiful', he would say, stroking the sleeve.

He also liked to keep me company whilst I worked on my computer. He would stand behind me running his hand through my hair – which is very thick – a loving gesture made in the past, as though marvelling at such abundance. I remembered that one day, many years ago, while he had made that gesture, I had bemoaned the appearance of a few grey hairs and he had said with great tenderness: 'Don't worry about them: they are a testament to your life.'

I don't think he recognized me as his wife anymore but he did see me as a familiar and reassuring presence. Sometimes he called me 'Mummy', but was unable to pronounce my name.

One evening, arriving home late after dinner with friends, I had found Francesco still awake. He watched me enter the room with some apprehension. I went close to the bed, and smoothing his brow I said, 'But don't you know who I am?' He shook his head. 'I am your wife…', I said tenderly. 'If only that were true!' he replied, with a look so full of love that sometimes I felt unworthy.

OUR ROUTINE DAILY activities had gradually lost all interest for Francesco. The magazines I bought for him were torn apart a page at a time, slowly, methodically. He had lost touch with the meaning of household fixtures. One day, urgently summoned to repair the WC, the plumber found a glass full of water and a large sponge in the tank. Another time, having seen a pot of cyclamen on the writing-desk, Francesco pulled out a handful of teaspoons from the kitchen drawer and carefully planted them one by one in the pot as though they were flowers. Among the variety of things that had disappeared was a certain large umbrella that had not been used for ages and that was found one day hanging from a hook on the window shutter. Then there was also the problem of the garden of our neighbour who lived below us, into which Francesco used to chuck out all his rubbish. I will always remember the night when, waking suddenly, I had found Francesco wandering around without his incontinence pad and had discovered with horror that the item in question was dangling from the branch of a rose bush below! In the middle of the night, under pelting rain, I had to go down on tiptoe so as not to wake my neighbour and free it from the thorns. Nevertheless, I noticed that nothing appeared to happen by chance. Each action seemed to be part of a well-defined plan. Thus, during meals that he normally ate with pleasure and appetite, Francesco would suddenly turn rigid when confronted by a sliced banana. These round slices became an architectural element for him and he placed them methodically around the edge of his plate, pouring a glass of water into the middle. Nothing would have persuaded him to eat those slices. As all round slices produced the same reaction in him, we had to cut the food into other shapes.

In time, even eating became a problem. Francesco had greater difficulties in swallowing his food and the time spent at table stretched endlessly. From the very beginning I had wanted us to have our meals together and for a long time – on my insistence – Francesco ate unaided using his knife and fork properly. But when the swallowing problems increased I had to change our menu and serve soups and purées. Nevertheless, he often choked dreadfully so that our meals took place in an atmosphere of great stress. His fork, now become dangerous, was replaced by a spoon. Finally, seated beside him, I had to feed him myself.

WE SUFFERED INTENSELY from loneliness during those years. As with all mental illnesses, Alzheimer's instils fear in people. I think that Francesco's friends were ill at ease when they came to visit, unsure of how to behave. I was deeply hurt, although I could well understand the reasons for their estrangement. Naturally there was never a lack of friendly telephone calls, but Francesco was of a sociable nature and he had always loved having friends in. I think he suffered greatly from their absence. When the bell rang, he would always get up and accompany me to the door, welcoming the guests with a handshake and a smile, and when they left the apartment he was the first to get to his feet. Once we had a visit from Lucky's relatives and Francesco was thrilled to be surrounded by so many people, albeit unknown. When they left, he started to walk around anxiously from one room to the other, asking disappointedly: 'But where are our friends?'

At the beginning of his illness Francesco was often prey to hallucinations: in the evening, for him, our living-room became crowded with guests. For these 'evening visitors' he would lay extra places at the table and got very cross if I removed them. Later I learned to let him do as he wished and often we ate at a table laid for six.

However, despite his pleasure in company, Francesco could not bear confusion and noise. He had been most upset when Myrto, a childhood friend of mine, came from Greece to spend a few days with us. At first he had followed with some interest the game of patience that Myrto had set out to play with him. But when we began to get busy laying the table and putting flowers into vases, I saw his face suddenly darken. He followed us around with a hostile expression. 'What's wrong,

Francesco, aren't you feeling well?' I asked. 'How can I feel well with all the confusion you two are creating!' I had not heard him give such a pertinent reply for ages and this gave me a happy feeling, despite his evident discomfort.

FRANCESCO NEVER LOST some of his old habits, such as going to sit in the kitchen when the cooking aromas wafted out. 'He is checking on me', Darshana used to laugh. He was also very aware of Darshana's duties towards him and used to hold his hand when they sat down together on the sofa to leaf through a magazine. One day when Darshana had tried to free himself from Francesco's grip to answer my call, he became angry and rebelled vigorously. Looking at me with the same dictatorial expression he had in the past, he protested: 'But Darshana works for *me*…!'

Holding hands gave him a sense of great security and when he parted from Darshana's he would immediately seize mine.

BEFORE HIS ILLNESS, Francesco used to rise very early, sometimes even before dawn. Despite the sleeping pills he took every night he did not sleep much. I remember being worried about this permanent insomnia but he assured me that those were the hours when he felt at his most creative, and that he enjoyed the silence that reigned over the house during those moments. During our trips across the Sahara he had taught me to experience the very same pleasure in those hours just before sunrise, a magic and solemn time in the silence of the desert.

When in Rome, Francesco alternated his activities during that time between the computer, on which he had installed various graphic programs, and games of patience which, he said, because of their repetitiveness left a space in which his mind was free to soar in search of new ideas and new plans. Sometimes I would get up and try to get him to come back to bed, but he did not listen because for him the day had already begun, and it was with a feeling of guilt that I returned to the warmth of the blankets.

Playing patience had always been a challenge. It was difficult to win because Francesco's system did not allow for easy victory and he had designed his own method that allowed him the chance to cheat three times. Many were the occasions in our camper or on our transatlantic crossings taking us to the States or to Canada that we had passed the time this way.

Now I encouraged Francesco to handle the cards once again, helping him to set them out in columns. But soon I realized that he could no longer follow the rules of the game and did not know how or why to make the moves. At first, he was able to recognize the numbers but when this capacity vanished, he began to line up the cards according to colour. For a long period he managed to distinguish between the red and the black and, sometimes, purposefully, I made mistakes to force him to put the cards in their right place.

And so, in the evening, sipping a glass of wine to herald the end of the day, we had the cards to keep us company. At times, irritated, he would tear one up, but I always had a pack in store so as not to interrupt our ritual.

Chapter Sixteen

One morning in December, with no forewarning, Francesco had his first epilepsy crisis. It started with a piercing scream, as he came out of the bathroom, followed by a fall. He remained prone for a long time, his eyes rolled back, his limbs rigid, his breathing laboured. We dared not move him fearing he had had a stroke, but Roberta, fortunately still at home when I rang her, was quick to recognize the symptoms, and gave me instructions on how to deal with the situation now and in the future. When we finally put Francesco to bed, he remained for a long while staring fixedly, red in the face, his eyes wide open and full of terror, not recognising his surroundings. He later fell into a deep sleep, his breathing still laboured but gradually becoming more regular, and when he woke an hour later he was his normal self again.

Despite this crisis, Roberta did not deem it necessary to initiate new medicines. 'It could be an isolated episode', she reassured me, 'we'll see if it happens again.' But for us this meant yet another anxiety; the fear of a new crisis; the constant pricking up of our ears to catch the first cry; the Valium injection to hand, and for me the terror, when out of the house, of hearing my mobile ring.

LITTLE BY LITTLE the disease had inexorably taken over our home. The discipline imposed at the beginning had started to disintegrate. The illness was stronger and outweighed any long term solution. In those days I had started to feel really afraid, and begun to lose my sense of security and the feeling that despite all I was on top of the situation, which had helped me to cope so far. I was now living in a state of permanent alarm. Furthermore, it seemed to me that the last fragile thread that linked me to Francesco was about to break. In fact, not only did he not recognize me now but he could also no longer understand what I was saying. For instance, he did not know what I meant when I said, 'Lift your foot so I can put your shoe on', 'Put on your dressing gown'. We had to take his foot and put it into the shoe and lift his arm to the armhole, and often he resisted strongly, pushing away the dressing gown and trying to remove his shoes.

We had had to give up Francesco's morning bath one day when he refused to get out of the tub, clinging terrified to the handle of the shower. It took more than an hour for Darshana and me to convince him that he was in no danger. The problem of how best to deal with the morning wash then arose.

Then one day, I had an idea. I remembered that in our last camper, a Volkswagen van in which, contrary to the roomy Dodge used for our Saharan crossings, space was restricted, we had put a large photo development tray on the bathroom floor. This tray contained all our sanitary fittings and had proved very useful. Its edge was only ten centimetres high and I thought that Francesco would easily be able to step into it with a little help. I immediately started the rounds of photographic material suppliers and, after many enquiries – because development techniques had now changed and been modernized – I found what I wanted: a 60 x 70 centimetre tray. In the morning we laid it in front of the basin and, with the help of a large soapy sponge, were able to give our patient a thorough wash.

FRANCESCO INCREASINGLY NEEDED my care, my presence and my attention. He was now unable to speak; not even the simplest words came to him anymore, and I was under the impression that he had given up trying altogether. He had more and more retreated into silence. He also seemed to have no wish to communicate with the outside world and his listless gaze was turned inwards, where perhaps he saw a more luminous reality. He kept his eyes closed, even when not asleep. Fearing the light might disturb him, I had moved his armchair so that he was turned away from the window. But despite this, he kept his eyes tightly shut as though to bear out his absence from our world.

He only glanced distractedly at the television, and often reacted to sounds by turning his head to the opposite side. He also walked with increasing difficulty and his balance was more and more unstable. One day, when he was coming up the stairs with me, he lost his balance and bent so far backwards that he fell, sliding down the flight of stairs and hitting his head against the front door. I thought he was dead. Hearing my cries for help, Darshana came to my rescue and together we managed to lift Francesco up and get him home. Miraculously he only had a grazed elbow but it was bleeding heavily. I ran to the nearest pharmacy, and I remember that on the way I was racked by violent sobs of frustration, conscious of the near tragedy and the realization of my growing helplessness.

Six years had gone by...

THE PROGRESSION OF the disease and Francesco's inability to cope with even the most basic functions of daily life placed both on me and on Darshana a heavy burden of stress that sometimes became unbearable. Each new problem drained a little more of my energy and my resistance. Ahead I could only see dead ends: when one road opened another one closed. I cannot deny that I lived moments of deep despair when a voice inside me cried 'Let's get it over!' but I shut it out because, of course, I did not want it to end. This was now my life: moments of distress interwoven with others of intense joy resulting from a brief recognition, a sudden smile repaying me for all my hardships. I was no stranger to anxiety but I no longer knew what boredom meant, because every minute of my day was taken up. I lived for a purpose, for someone. Seldom in the past had I known such a fullness of life, with no doubts as to the reason for my actions.

In the almost seven years of Francesco's illness I had never been sick, not even for a day. And, alongside that great strength, love also grew in me, a sentiment that was different from our initial relationship with all its qualms, its vulnerability, its fear of disappointing or making mistakes: this new emotion had the solidity of a rock. It blossomed through giving rather than receiving; it was reciprocal but expected nothing in return. It was perhaps the purest expression of love.

I felt the tenderness and compassion one feels for a retarded, invalid and totally dependent child, and perhaps something more because Francesco never asked for anything, one had to interpret his needs and, in a certain sense, create his life, a life in which he had no say but that he accepted blindly and totally. Such a deep mutual feeling helped to smooth over many of the most dramatic aspects of the disease. We spoke with gestures, handshakes, smiles and Francesco expressed his love by gently touching my face, stroking my hair the way he used to do in the past. Our roles were now totally reversed. He called me 'Mummy' more and more often. He would say to Darshana: 'Where is my mother?' and I, as with a child, gave him orders: 'Do this, come here, sit down', and he would obey without question.

THERE WAS ANOTHER epilepsy crisis a year after the first, followed by others, more and more frequent, a week later. They began as the first one with a cry of anguish, then his whole body would become rigid until relief came through a Valium injection. Roberta had warned me that, if the crises became too frequent, a treatment based on barbiturates would be necessary. 'These are drugs that can damage the liver, but sometimes they are essential', she had told me.

Taking the barbiturates was the last straw for Francesco. From one week to another, his cognitive capacities gradually deteriorated and his reactions were slower. He was in a permanent state of drowsiness where even simply eating became a major problem and swallowing was more and more difficult and hazardous. He could now only manage puréed food. Sometimes we had to skip a meal when the effort to eat became too much for him. We also had to give up our walks because of his frailty. This prolonged immobility had soon caused bed sores. Despite daily massages and soothing ointments, his silicone cushion and other devices, we had not been able to prevent lesions on his back and heels. Francesco did not seem to suffer and that was a positive aspect. It seemed to me that his pain threshold was considerably higher and he did not suffer greatly either from the heat of that exceptionally torrid summer.

ONE DAY, DARSHANA suddenly announced that he could not cope any longer alone and that he needed help. I too was conscious of the increasing difficulties he encountered in getting Francesco out of bed, leading him to the bathroom and helping him take a little exercise to keep his blood circulation active. So I started to look around for extra help.

Among the applicants was Roni, a Sri Lankan girl, young, strong and with a serene expression, who took up her duties immediately. She came early in the morning and left late in the evening, after having helped Darshana to put Francesco to bed.

Roni's arrival inevitably brought about deep changes in our lifestyle. I felt I was a stranger in my own home and retired more and more to my little study. Darshana seemed satisfied and I rejoiced at their apparent good co-operation because Roni's presence had really become essential. Francesco was given a strip-wash in his bed every morning, a task that was particularly difficult because of his resistance. Unfortunately, together with Roni, another unwelcome guest entered our home: the wheel-chair.

The rhythm of our day had changed to fit in with the new needs. I tried to keep up the harmony and serenity as before but it was becoming ever more difficult. We lived in a pervading tense atmosphere that I could not interpret.

After lunch, when Francesco went to rest in his bedroom, Darshana usually locked himself in his room and Roni rested on a deck-chair in the kitchen. I then had the use of the living-room, the heart of the house and of our life, but above all I had the comfort of my little study.

I had added the study shortly after Francesco's illness began, and, when I closed the door behind me, it took on amazing dimensions. Near my desk was the telephone that connected me with the outside world; there was my computer for work and research, but also as a means via the Internet to communicate with my clients. On the wall hung my favourite photographs: four large groups of flowers in black and white solarized by Francesco and myself when we had a photo lab. A photograph of a smiling Francesco, towering over a group of women at the market in Bobo Dioulasso. Another one of me, a tiny silhouette, against the background of the Sahara and, just a speck on the horizon, our Dodge.

I was the queen here. No one entered except Francesco at the times he came to visit. As the study was windowless a large fan kept me company with its subtle whirr. Here I could finally find peace, I could unwind, I could leave behind for a while all the grief that had now invaded our house. For a few hours I could be myself again.

I HAD GRADUALLY noticed evident changes in Darshana's behaviour. He seemed to have delegated all the responsibilities for the apartment to Roni. Now it was she who took care of all the daily chores such as washing, ironing, cooking. Darshana continually asked permission to go out on various pretexts, so that although I had two people in my service, only one was actually working. I did not complain: what was important was that Francesco was properly cared for.

Although by now Francesco's epileptic crises had ceased so that I felt more reassured, on the other hand the atmosphere of the apartment was gradually worsening. I was puzzled as to how to face the situation because in actual fact neither Roni nor Darshana had complained about the other, and the days had passed by without any apparent clashes between them. Until one day I came home to find Roni in tears. I immediately thought she had received bad news from her husband in Sri Lanka, or that there was some other serious problem, so I questioned her. In between sobs she told me that

Darshana had treated her badly, that he had insulted her – and that that morning he had even threatened her with a knife. I was aghast and deeply upset. Nothing had prepared me for this. The whole precarious wall I had built around the disease depended on the good co-operation of my two helpers, and now this was suddenly collapsing. Roni could not cope alone and neither could Darshana. 'I can manage perfectly well on my own', he had declared stubbornly when Roni, resolute in her decision to leave was packing her bags. But I knew he could never manage, as experience had proved, and I started to study the option of finding temporary respite care for Francesco while I looked for an adequate solution.

AND THIS IS how the Villa Flavia was chosen. Francesco could spend a month or two there while I decided how best to face the situation. I told Darshana that the doctor had prescribed treatments that could only be carried out in a clinic. As Francesco's stay there might be lengthy, I advised him to look for another job. I was not worried about his future because he had a wealthy uncle in Rome who would always welcome him and who helped him, although retaining large amounts of money from his salary for a house that they planned to build together in Sri Lanka. The date of Francesco's admission in the clinic was decided. And that is how the distress and sorrow of this phase started, marking my third betrayal.

Francesco must have understood that an important change was about to take place because he suddenly became extremely restless. He had begun to keep his eyes open again and to look around him once more. After weeks of almost total immobility he had even started to take a few steps around the house. Obviously my remorse grew correspondingly.

I tried to convince myself that this was only a temporary solution, but deep inside I sensed that it might become permanent. In my little study one day, trying to escape such sad thoughts by attacking a new translation, I suddenly saw Francesco on Darshana's arm coming towards me, with his eyes wide open, his sweet smile and such a knowing look in his eyes that it rent my heart. Then he lifted his hand and laid it on my head. It was his way of saying good-bye to me.

MY FRIEND JOAN came the next morning to pick us up in her large car. Francesco could barely stand up, as though he had suddenly surrendered all his strength.

The road to the clinic seemed endless. As Francesco stepped from the car, he fell flat in front of the entrance. The head nurse, who ran towards us with a wheel-chair, reproached me for having waited so long before bringing him, admonishing that a man in his condition should have been entrusted long ago to professional care. Francesco was taken to his room where he closed his eyes again.

The following days were gruelling. Francesco violently rejected his new surroundings, stubbornly refusing to adapt to the new situation and sometimes even refusing to eat. He retired into silence and no longer replied to my questions. He did not even open his eyes when spoken to. I visited him every day, often at lunch time to help him eat, to comfort him with the sound of my voice. But no smile rewarded me anymore and sometimes he seemed even to withdraw from physical contact. He had also grown so painfully thin that the skin of his face stretched taut over his prominent nose and his long neck.

I suffered intensely. Whenever I planned to stay at home to finish a job, I would find myself in the car on my way to the clinic. Only there could I find peace. Sometimes it was the rest hour and I would sit near Francesco in the silent room, the only sound being the buzz of the vibrating equipment used to prevent bed sores.

Francesco did not seem to suffer physical pain because he never complained. I kept telling myself that this was the only possible solution for him, but it was only when bronchitis set in and then turned to pneumonia that I was finally convinced. The clinic had all the necessary equipment, immediately available, to relieve the catarrh blocking his lungs, to give him the oxygen he needed when his breathing got shallow and to stabilize his dwindling blood pressure. One Sunday, not having found him in the communal lounge where the patients gathered for recreation in the afternoons, I went up to his room. He was sitting in an armchair, one arm connected to a drip and tied to the arm of the chair to keep it from falling. His breathing had become very laboured. Although his temperature had gone down, he was in a state of extreme weakness. The doctor told me that he had not eaten for two days and that they wanted to begin force-feeding. I strongly opposed this, deeming that Francesco had already suffered enough. I tried to take his hand in mine to infuse in him some of my strength as I had often done in the past, but he withdrew it at once. I tried again, but with his free hand he pushed it away. I left with my heart heavier than ever.

Early the next morning, while I was getting ready to go to the clinic, a telephone call arrived telling me that Francesco had died.

NEVER COULD I have imagined the void that Francesco's death would leave in me. It seemed that suddenly all my energy accumulated over the last years had dissipated. It was not only the psychological pain of the loss of a loved one I was experiencing but also a physical sense of amputation. I seemed no longer able to walk. I was like an invalid used to leaning on a stick who finds himself suddenly without support. When I travelled by bus people would suddenly offer me their seats.

The great undertaking that had given a meaning to my life for more than six years was suddenly no more. I had to recreate my life again starting from scratch.

It was a long and difficult journey, and I thought at first that I would never make it back up again. I still found it unbearable to return to the empty apartment with its overwhelming silence; to sleep next to an empty bed; to eat in a cold and hostile kitchen. Sometimes I used to prepare dishes that I did not even eat, in order just to smell their aroma.

I grieved for all the times we had been together; the happy as well as the dark, because we had lived them so intensely, because together we had been able to overcome, day by day, the hardships and the suffering caused by the unforgiving and devastating disease that is Alzheimer's. I was nostalgic for the precious days of being at Francesco's side, even though at times he was not always aware of my presence, and the strength I had derived just from giving and the joy therein. I realized that, in the end, our journey together instead of a grievous duty had turned into a love story.

Chapter Seventeen

Our meeting is just over. Small groups are forming for last conversations, for an exchange of opinions and experiences. A young girl is in tears, she has just been told that her father has Alzheimer's. Someone now recounts an episode that he did not dare tell the group. Others listen in silence. A strong bond of solidarity holds together these people who are united in the same battle against the disease. But they come from the meeting feeling more serene, encouraged. For a short while they have felt less alone.

Like them, I relive all the phases of my journey. I feel that I too belong to this community, and I speak of resignation, patience, understanding and compassion, but above all of love. And thus it seems that I am giving some sense to Francesco's sufferings and that, in helping them, I am making him live a little longer beside me.